Roadside Amusements
an imprint of Chamberlain Bros.
a member of Penguin Group (USA) Inc.
New York

Roadside Amusements
Published by the Penguin Group
Penguin Group (USA) Inc., 375 Hudson Street, New York, New York 10014, USA
Penguin Group (Canada), 10 Alcorn Avenue, Toronto, Ontario, Canada M4V 3B2 (a
division of Pearson Penguin Canada Inc.)
Penguin Books Ltd, 80 Strand, London WC2R 0RL, England
Penguin Ireland, 25 St Stephen's Green, Dublin 2, Ireland (a division of Penguin
Books Ltd)
Penguin Group (Australia), 250 Camberwell Road, Camberwell, Victoria 3124,
Australia
(a division of Pearson Australia Group Pty Ltd)
Penguin Books India Pvt Ltd, 11 Community Centre, Panchsheel Park, New
Delhi–110 017, India
Penguin Group (NZ), Cnr Airborne and Rosedale Roads, Albany, Auckland, New
Zealand
(a division of Pearson New Zealand Ltd)
Penguin Books (South Africa) (Pty) Ltd, 24 Sturdee Avenue, Rosebank, Johannesburg
2196, South Africa

Penguin Books Ltd, Registered Offices: 80 Strand, London WC2R 0RL, England

Big Daddy's Zubba Bubba BBQ
    p. cm
ISBN 1-59609-012-X
1. Barbecue cookery
TX840.B3B545 2005   2004061374
641.5'784—dc22

Printed in China
10 9 8 7 6 5 4 3 2 1

Book design by Mike Rivilis

Contents

Foreword
Remus Powers, Ph.B.
(Doctor of Barbecue Philosophy)

Ihave seen the road ahead and it is BARBECUE! It used to be that barbecue was strictly a Bubba thing, and before that it was thought to be a plantation thing. Not so today. Not so tomorrow, either. Barbecue is here to stay in a backyard near you, in restaurants everywhere, and in the already huge competition circuit that gets bigger every year. If you are looking for a book that will introduce you to today's world of barbecue and make you a part of it, you've found it.

Big Daddy's Zubba Bubba BBQ will find favor with a variety of cooks and readers. Whether you're a master of the pit or a beginner in need of a basic barbecue starter kit, you'll find tips and recipes in here that run the gamut from hot and fast backyard grilling to slow and low authentic barbecue.

Here you'll get a wealth of recipes from cooks at barbecue cooking contests and food festivals across the country. The editors did the traveling and got the recipes for you. I know you'll have fun reading this book, cooking from it, and meeting some of the many characters who share a love of barbecue, cooking, and fun.

Over the past half a century or so I've met or heard about many Big Daddies. A memorable one was in Des

Moines, Iowa, several years ago. The late Big Daddy Isaac Seymour Jr. made sauces so hot you'd wonder if you could make it to the next bite alive. One of his hottest was appropriately named "Emergency Room," and he wouldn't let you try it without first getting your signature on a liability waiver.

Then there's Big Daddy Jean-Pierre Gelinas and Big Mama Loretta, chef-proprietors of Yazoo City Real American Food on Long Island. Dang, can they make sauce! I swear they ought to get a presidential medal for the sauce they call "Jump into an Open Grave." Boiled habañero peppers are the first ingredient, but the peppers were slightly tamed with pineapple juice, vinegar, and some secret spices, bringing sweat to your brow and a smile to your face.

There's another Big Daddy in Florence, Alabama, who makes a barbecue sauce so hot and wonderful that it's worth the expense of driving from your place to his place just to get the sauce. It's one of those hot ones that starts sweet and follows with a WHAP in your mouth.

Yes, there's a theme here: Big Daddy, wherever you may find him, is HOT!

Likewise you'll find that the Big Daddy of this book delivers hot views, hot barbecue, and the best and hottest tips on how to build your own Big Daddy reputation.

As far as I'm concerned you can't have too many books about barbecue. While the quality of what's available today varies from mediocre to excellent, I haven't found one yet that hasn't had something new to teach me. This one in particular benefits from being a collective effort, a harvest of recipes from a community of barbecuers, and it lands on the excellent end of the continuum.

Big Daddy's Zubba Bubba BBQ hits the mark in title and content. It cuts a wide swath across the culinary landscape, but mainly it's about how to cook barbecue and what to serve with it—all in an entertaining format that goes beyond a simple presentation of recipes.

Just like Big Daddy, today's world of barbecue is big, bodacious, and bursting with Bubbas. I also know Bubba. A friend in Lynchburg, Tennessee, once told me, "If you don't remember a fellow's name down here in Dixie, just call him 'Bubba,' and better than fifty percent of the time you'll get it right." It's not that a lot of Southerners carry the legal name of "Bubba." Rather it's a term of endearment akin to "buddy." Of course it only applies to men. I've heard the term "Bubbette" applied to women, but mostly with tongue in cheek. There are other terms of endearment for women— "honey," "girlfriend," and "darling," to name a few.

What I like about this book is the variety of culinary talents and recipes it embraces. The editors went to a lot of trouble to seek out and find barbecuers from all over the country and ask them for a favorite recipe or two to share with you in this book. Some contributors are grand champions; some are accomplished backyard barbecuers; some would rather judge than compete—but all love barbecue and are willing to share some of their secrets with you.

There was a time in the history of barbecue when regional differences were more distinct than today. The notion of several barbecue regions with signature styles of cooking and seasonings has enjoyed credence and popularity for years, but my problem with regional groupings today is they don't cover the entire world of barbecue in America, let alone the rest of the planet. They also tend to say more about how it used to be in a region, and less about how it is today. Sure, there's Memphis, Texas, Kansas City, South Carolina, eastern and western North Carolina, Kentucky, Oklahoma, and other parts of the country where you can find a predictable style of barbecue, but the landscape is changing. Instead of seven or more "regions," Barbecue Country is virtually everywhere. This is not to say that it's OK to deprive yourself of a barbecue mutton sandwich with burgoo in Owensboro, Kentucky, or that it's OK to never eat a pulled pork sandwich in North Carolina or Tennessee, South Carolina or Alabama, or that if you miss the barbecue brisket, sausage, and ribs at Luling City Market or Louie Mueller's or Kreutz Market in Texas you haven't missed anything. Lordy, no! You owe it to yourself to take a Barbecue Odyssey someday through the cities and states that made American barbecue famous and spawned the barbecue craze that has spread across the country.

Thanks to the gifted pitmasters in traditional barbecue country, the entire American landscape today is Barbecue Country. Wherever you are, if you can't find good barbecue in a nearby restaurant, backyard, or festival, you needn't worry. With *Big Daddy's Zubba Bubba BBQ* in hand you can cook your own bodacious batch of barbecue. When you don't feel like cooking just put "barbecue order" in your search engine and shop the Net. Home delivery from Texas, Memphis, Kansas City, Alabama, or elsewhere to your door may be pricey, but when you crave the real thing the price is only money. I predict, however, that after you master some of the recipes in this book and adopt them as your own, you'll do less outsourcing and more home cooking. Nothing beats the freshness and tender loving care of home-cooked barbecue and side dishes.

Keep this book on hand for everyday inspiration as well as those times when you're looking for recipes to entertain your guests with something fun and different. Write notes in the margins when you try a recipe and make changes to suit your taste. If your personal copy of *Big Daddy's Zubba Bubba BBQ* isn't soiled, written in, and sprinkled with sauce stains a year from now, then you haven't been paying attention!

Introduction

Here's the thing. If you take meat and fire and mix the two, the end result is gonna taste good. You get a burger at a picnic, straight from the grocer's freezer, and from steer to flame, it'll get the job done. Thing is, that's not barbecue. It's good, and with some ketchup and a beer it'll do for a meal, but there's something missing between the hamburger buns, and I don't mean the cheese. You just had yourself a grilled burger, and while there ain't nothing wrong with it, you at least deserve to know that there's a whole world out there, beyond the "sizzle, flip, remove" life of the backyard grill jockey.

So let me tell y'all a little something about Barbecue. Barbecue, or BBQ, if you've got a thing against vowels, is more than just fire and meat, bigger than charcoal, hickory, and propane, and better that some sauce doused over a piece of beef . . . or pork. . . . Now, I'm not saying it can't be any of those things, but just understand that when you throw your dinner on the rack, you've got choices. You can cook it—let it sit on one side, then turn it over until the middle reaches your preferred shade of red (or white)—or you can barbecue it.

BBQ (now you know where I stand) is a way of life, a sweet, savored style of cooking that at its best takes hours to get just right, and finds company and canned beverages to fill the time, if you get my drift. It's got accents from across the country—Louisiana, Texas, Carolina, Kansas City, and Memphis, to name a few. I even hear the folks in New York City are spending thousands and thousands every year to try and get filters set up so they can join the fun . . . at least that's one thing that they've got their priorities set in the right direction on. BBQ is a universal, with great Asian and Caribbean recipes too, as if somewhere right after fire and the wheel men on every continent all shared an epiphany to marinate. That's where the Zubba Bubba comes in. Some will claim reign over the BBQ kingdom, as if their meat don't stink after being left out in the sun for too long, and I get asked all the time, "Big Daddy, where's the best BBQ at?" Folks, I'll tell you like it is, the only time I turn my nose up is when the Barbecue Festival comes into town . . . and that's only so I can follow the smoke to the source. Zubba Bubba is a celebration of the best barbecue has to offer, and that means the best from all over.

Now, I know what you're gonna tell me: "Big Daddy, we don't have a dual-exhaust smoker. Big Daddy, our city's clean air act calls the best-smelling smoke in the world pollution and we could get a fine for twelve hours of charcoal cooking. Big Daddy, we don't have the time." It's this last one that gets me most, by the way. Not everyone can slow-cook their meat to perfection, I understand it. Some folks don't have the equipment (although we've got some nifty ways inside to give you a taste of what you're missing), some don't have the taste, some don't have the smarts–this I can work with. In fact, half the reason I put this book together was to lend a clue to the guys who *think* they know how to barbecue but who would rather ask directions from a gas-station attendant before admitting they need help around the grill. You know who you are.

Some of you are my neighbors, whom I've seen do downright dangerous things in the name of my favorite cuisine. The good news is, there's help for those who ask for it, but if you don't have the time, then, son, you're missing out.

BBQ is all about taking the time. I don't care if you're grilling, smoking, or if you've just finished rubbing your sticks together fast enough to get a campfire going and now you want to reward yourself with a steak and a beverage. Any carnivore can throw his dinner into a pit. Heck, the cavemen figured that one out millions of years ago. It wasn't until man evolved, and came up with his first secret rub recipe that it all started tasting good. This whole book is about making the best with what you have, and if all you got is a hand-me-down hibachi, that'll do. This first chapter here covers some barbecue basics, including cuts of meats, types of grills, and food safety.

Chapter 1 offers some all-purpose barbecue seasoning recipes, all of which can be made in advance and kept on hand for whatever you will.

Chapters 2-8 contain recipes for main courses ranging from the familiar to the exotic; you'll also find interesting twists on barbecue standards. Now, listen, I know some guys who won't even tell their wives what goes in the ribs, but Big Daddy has got it covered. I've called on the best of the best to help me put together what you now hold before you, prize-winning recipes from championship teams around the country. My mission in life, right after eating and drinking (and right before more drinking and more eating), is to get you to try as many of these great recipes on your own as your body can handle, and maybe learn a few tricks of the trade. Heck, I hope you take what I've got in here and use it to make your own recipes, slap your name on it, and impress the hell out of your wife or girlfriend (or both).

The final chapters focus on side dishes, drinks, and desserts that are superb accompaniments to any barbecue meal. The recipes in each chapter are presented from the least to most complicated.

So put the beer down—don't worry, it'll keep cold, that's what the cozy is for—and let's begin with a short refresher course, Barbecue 101 if you will. For all you experienced grillers out there, go ahead and skip to Chapter 1, I won't be insulted. For the rest of you, fire up the coals and let ole Big Daddy come show you how it's done. . . .

Barbecue Basics
Cuts of Meat

If you're a low-carber or think those tree-huggin' vegetarians should be cooked on a spit, then meat is your best friend. There's plenty to choose from, too. Poultry lovers can find easy success grillin' any part of the chicken, turkey, or game—as long as the bird is cut up. Pork, particularly chops, ribs, and tenders, cooks up real nice over a fire. But when it comes to cooking outdoors, beef reigns supreme, in my not-so-humble opinion.

The U.S. Department of Agriculture (USDA) grades meat according to quality level. There are eight possible grades, but the ones you'll be most interested in are the top three: USDA Prime (restaurant grade), Choice (the most popular consumer grade), and Select.

The three lowest grades of meat—Utility, Cutter, and Canner—are usually used to make ground beef and other meat items, such as frankfurters (which makes this cookbook even more valuable when your kids demand hot dogs for dinner every night).

Regardless of their USDA report card, some cuts of meat are naturally more tender than others. For instance, cuts from the less-used muscles along the back of the animal—the rib and loin sections—will always be more tender than those from the more active muscles, such as the shoulder, flank, and leg.

Since the tenderest cuts compose just a small percentage of any beef or lamb carcass, they are in greatest demand and are therefore more costly than other cuts. If money's tight (or you're a tightwad, like me), barbecuing offers a natural detour: marinating for several hours prior to barbecuing tenderizes any cut of meat. Barbecuing also frees you from always investing in the leanest cuts of meat; in fact, fat is a friend of the grill—not only does it help prevent meat from burning, most of the fat drips through the grill and away from your belly during the cooking process.

There are literally hundreds of different beef cuts, but the most popular retail cuts are:

- **Forequarter steaks**—chuck blade steak, beef rib steak (with or without bone), rib eye, skirt steak
- **Forequarter roasts**—pot roast, beef chuck seven-bone pot roast, large end roast, round rump boneless roast
- **Hindquarter steaks**—flank steak, round tip steak, top round steak, bottom round steak, eye round steak
- **Hindquarter loin steaks**—top loin steak, T-bone steak, porterhouse steak, tenderloin steak, sirloin steak

Outdoor Cooking Methods

For some, "barbecue" is used as a catchall term for any food cooked outdoors, whether it's smoked or heated directly over an open flame. Barbecue can also refer to something cooked on one of those newfangled indoor grills, as well as things that are lathered with barbecue sauce and baked or broiled in the oven. To purists, barbecuing in the oven may be heresy, but in my view, there's no shame (or significant loss of flavor) in oven-prepared barbecue; to prove my point, I've scattered a few recipes using the indoor method throughout the book. They're great when you're hankering for that rich barbecue flavor on a rainy day.

Outdoor cooking enthusiasts can choose from a wide array of barbecue methods, ranging from throwing wood and a lit match into a hole in the ground to cooking on the gourmet equivalent of a Hummer with a hot tub. Here are some of the most popular outdoor cooking devices:

Grilling—Show me a suburbanite without a barbecue grill, and I'll show you someone who should move back to the city. Backyard grills are sold through so many retail outlets these days that I've lost count—Home Depot, Wal-Mart, Sears, Kmart, Lowe's, appliance stores, and outdoor furniture stores, to name a few. My local grocery store carries grills on a seasonal basis. And, like every other consumer product in the universe, barbecue grills can be purchased over the Internet.

Backyard grills come in many brands but fall into two general categories—gas and those that burn charcoal, wood, or both. Gas grills come in a variety of sizes and range in price from about $100 for a no-frills version to $1,500 or more for a stylish high-tech model that can accommodate food for fifteen people. Some of these babies are equipped with rotisserie, as well.

Most gas grills are mounted on a rolling cart, have a cast-iron cover, and at least two grilling surfaces; moderately priced grills typically include a side burner, which is great for warming up sauce or baked beans. For all you tailgate party animals, Weber has come out with the Weber Q grill, which has a mini propane tank (I'm still waiting for someone to invent a tailgate grill that includes a little fridge for beer). Regular backyard gas grills use larger, refillable tanks, or you can choose a model that gets hooked to a gas line in your house. While gas grilling offers the cleanest, quickest way to grill food, you do sacrifice some of that smoky flavor (although a good marinade can compensate). A big advantage to gas grilling is the ability to control temperature precisely, thanks to built-in temperature gauges. Gas grills have ignition starters that generate a spark, but in my experience, the igniter button is the first thing to break on a gas grill. Electronic starters are reportedly more reliable. Another feature to look for is stainless steel or coated cast-iron grates, which tend to heat more evenly than porcelain-coated steel grates.

Charcoal must be started thirty to sixty minutes in advance of cooking to create burning embers that will heat food evenly. Although there is more cleanup involved, these grills tend to be smaller and more portable. City dwellers can buy a mini grill for their balcony, and many parks have permanent charcoal grills in their picnic areas. When shopping for a charcoal cooker, look for an adjustable grill surface. You can pick up a little one- or two-season grill for under $20 or spend $1,000 for a high-end model warranted for ten years.

Charcoal grills have the capability to impart smoky flavors, which is enhanced by mixing wood chips onto the coals, or using hardwood instead of charcoal for fuel. Pecan wood, for example, imparts a moderately fruity taste and is one of the most versatile woods for briskets, roasts, chops, steaks, and poultry. Alder and cherry have a more delicate flavor and are ideal for grilling fish and poultry. Mesquite, by contrast, has a very strong flavor that has become popular for grilling meat and chicken for fajitas; simply toss a handful of water-soaked mesquite chips over the bed of charcoal as it is heating up.

Smoking—Smoking means cooking food indirectly in the presence of a fire. It can be done in a covered charcoal grill if a pan of water is placed beneath the meat. Meats can also be smoked in a "smoker," which is an outdoor cooker especially designed for this purpose. Smoking is done much more slowly than grilling, so less tender meats benefit from this method and a natural smoke flavoring permeates the meat. The temperature in the smoker should be maintained at 250°F to 300°F for safety.

Pit Roasting—Pit roasting is cooking meat in a large, level hole dug in the earth. You'll need a quantity of hardwood equal to about two and one half times the volume of the pit. The hardwood is allowed to burn until the wood reduces and the pit is half filled with burning coals. This can require four to six hours of burning time. Pit roasting may require ten to twelve hours or more and is difficult to estimate. Remember to use a meat thermometer to determine the meat's safety and doneness (see next section). There are many variables, such as outdoor temperature, the size and thickness of the meat, and how fast the coals are cooking.

Food Safety Tips

Throughout this book—flagged by the attention-grabbing phrase BIG DADDY LOWDOWN—you'll find ways to lower the risk of poisoning your family and guests, along with my own insight, wit, and wisdom. The first rule of thumb is to always handle raw food as though it is contaminated with illness-causing bacteria ("pathogens" in scientific speak). This means keeping cold foods cold (below 40°F) and hot foods hot (above 140°F); washing your hands with soap and warm water after handling raw meat or poultry; and using separate platters, knives, spatulas, and other cooking utensils for uncooked and cooked foods. Here are some other important safety tips from the experts at the USDA's Food Safety and Inspection Service:

- When shopping, buy meats and poultry last, right before checkout. To guard against cross-contamination—which can happen when raw meat or poultry juices drip on other food—put packages of raw meat and poultry into plastic bags.
- At home, stick meat and poultry in the fridge immediately. Freeze poultry and ground meat, unless you'll be using it in the next day or two.
- Completely defrost meat and poultry before grilling so it cooks evenly. Thaw in the refrigerator or in sealed packages in cold water. You can safely defrost in a microwave, but only if the food is to be placed on the grill immediately.
- Meat and poultry cooked on a grill often browns very fast on the outside and can look done before it is, so use a food thermometer. Chicken parts should be cooked to 170°F; ground beef to 160°F; ground poultry to 165°F; beef, veal, lamb, roasts, and chops to 145°F; all cuts of pork to 160°F; and hot dogs to 165°F.
- Never partially grill meat or poultry and then finish cooking later. You're not mowing the lawn here.
- Keep cooked meats hot by setting them to the side of the grill rack, not directly over the coals where they can overcook.
- Refrigerate leftovers promptly in shallow containers. Discard any food left out more than two hours (one hour if the ambient temperature is above 90°F).

More Tips for Safe Grilling

- Never use a grill indoors. Place the grill at least ten feet away from your house or any building. Do not use the grill in a garage, breezeway, carport, or porch, or under any surface that can catch fire.
- Be sure the grill is on a level surface and well away from landscaping and hanging tree branches.
- With gas grills, check hoses for cracking, brittleness, holes, and leaks. Make sure there are no sharp bends in the hose or tubing. Always store the gas cylinder outside and away from the house.
- With charcoal grills, only use starter fluids designed for that purpose. Never use gasoline, and never add more liquid fuel after the fire has started or you might create a flash fire. Chimney starters can provide a safe, efficient method for starting charcoals without starter fluid. You can pick up one of these devices for about $12-$15.
- Be sure the fire is out when you are finished. For gas grills, turn off the control valves and the tank valve. Let the grill cool completely before you cover it. With a charcoal grill, replace the lid and close all vents. If you are going to dispose of the coals, be sure to soak them with water first or wait at least forty-eight hours.
- For protection while grilling, wear a heavy apron and an oven mitt that fits over your forearm. And don't forget that grills remain hot long after you have finished barbecuing.
  (Source: USDA)

1
Rubs and Sauces

I've said it before—what separates modern man from a Bronze Age hunter roasting his kill? Rubs and sauces, of course! These intense seasoning blends improve the taste of almost any cut of beef, chicken, or pork. You can control the heat by using slightly more or less chili pepper.

Dry rub can be rubbed or sprinkled on uncooked meat. Allow time for the meat juices to saturate the rub before cooking; you'll know it's ready to grill when the spices look wet on the surface of the meat.

If you barbecue as often as I do, you'll want to keep stashes of dry rub and sauce handy, although most of these recipes can be thrown together in ten minutes or less.

Big Daddy Lowdown: To keep from contaminating your stash, throw out any rub or sauce that falls off the meat during the seasoning process.

Darn-Good Dry Rub

You can vary this and the next recipe by substituting tablespoons for teaspoons. Store rub in an airtight spice jar or clean margarine container, and label. Shake well before each use.

4 teaspoons paprika
2 teaspoons salt
2 teaspoons onion powder

2 teaspoons ground black pepper
1 teaspoon cayenne pepper

Put all ingredients into an airtight container, seal, and shake well to mix. Allow seasoned meat to stand 20 to 30 minutes at room temperature, until rub appears wet.
Makes about 1/4 cup rub

Different Darn-Good Dry Rub

4 tablespoons paprika
2 teaspoons salt
2 teaspoons onion powder

2 teaspoons black pepper
2 teaspoons white pepper
1 teaspoon cayenne pepper

Put all ingredients into an airtight container, seal, and shake well to mix. Allow seasoned meat to stand 20 to 30 minutes at room temperature, until rub appears wet.
Makes about 1/2 cup rub

The Right-Way Rub

This rub offers just the right amount of spiciness for me; but of course, I like my meat to bite back. If you don't, make a milder rub by using 1/2 tablespoon of ground chili instead of a full tablespoon.

1 tablespoon ground red chili
2 teaspoons Hungarian paprika
1 teaspoon ground cumin
1 teaspoon ground coriander
1 teaspoon salt
1 teaspoon onion powder
1 teaspoon garlic powder

1/2 teaspoon dry mustard
1/2 teaspoon freshly ground
    black pepper
1/2 teaspoon dried thyme leaves
1/2 teaspoon curry powder
1/2 teaspoon ground allspice

Mix together all ingredients. Rub on meat, and refrigerate the night before smoking or barbecuing.
Makes about 1/4 cup rub

Budha's All-Purpose Meat Rub

I took a trip down to the Great Lenexa Barbecue Battle with some of my boys in the summer of '04, and Budha and his team, Budha Mangus, took the event to a whole other level. The food and partying that came out of their tent went above and beyond the call of duty, and for that, we salute them. As for their rub, to quote Budha, "If you rub your meat more than once . . . then you're just having a good time."

Budha uses this rub on just about everything from hamburgers to salmon. This recipe will make enough rub to get you through a competition, something Budha knows plenty about, having finished in the top five in almost a

Budha Mangus

Oklahoma Joe's - Kansas Speedway
May 31 - June 1, 2003

dozen events for everything from chicken to ribs to sausage. For home use, he cuts the recipe by 1/2 to 1/4. To control the heat, adjust the cayenne pepper (or replace cayenne pepper with habanero for that extra kick). Budha uses fresh dried peppers when he makes his, which makes a big difference.

3/4 cup coarse sea salt
1 1/2 cups brown sugar
1 1/2 cups granulated sugar
2 tablespoons cumin
2 tablespoons chili powder
2 tablespoons Hungarian paprika
2 tablespoons garlic powder
2 teaspoons black pepper

2 teaspoons ground cayenne pepper
2 teaspoons ground celery seed
1 teaspoon anise
1 teaspoon coriander
1 teaspoon Chinese five spice
2 teaspoons Mexican oregano
1 tablespoon MSG

Combine all ingredients in a glass or plastic bowl. Unused mixture can be stored in an airtight container.
Makes about 4 1/2 cups rub

River City Rubs

The boys at River City Rub compete on the KCBS contest circuit, and have racked up their share of awards. They bring their Memphis-style BBQ to anywhere from seven to ten events annually, and in the last two years they've taken home Grand Champion honors twice with their out-of-this-world ribs at the Ashland, Mississippi, State Championship. Their brisket ain't too shabby either, finishing second in 2004 at the American Royal Invitational in Kansas City.

These three rubs here are gonna knock your socks off. Use them for your own recipes if you like, just mix the ingredients, coat the meat, and let it stand—the longer the better. Whatever you do, make sure you save this page (go ahead and fold over the corner if you want—it's your book, you bought it), so you can come back to it when River City gets us rolling in the later chapters with their prizewinning chicken, pork, and ribs.

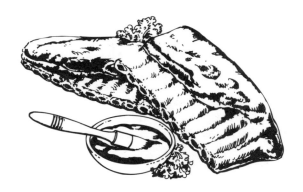

River City Pork Rub

1/2 cup paprika
1 tablespoon black pepper
1 tablespoon kosher salt
1 tablespoon cayenne pepper
1 tablespoon garlic powder

1 tablespoon garlic salt
1 tablespoon dry mustard
1 tablespoon ground cumin
Optional: 3 tablespoons packed
    brown sugar if you like it sweet

Makes about 1 cup rub

River City Chicken Rub

1 teaspoon sugar
1 teaspoon garlic powder
1 teaspoon onion powder
1 teaspoon cayenne pepper

1 teaspoon dry mustard
1 teaspoon sweet paprika
1 tablespoon kosher salt

Makes about 3 tablespoons rub, but since everything is measured in equal parts, you can use tablespoons instead of teaspoons and make a little less than 1/2 cup

River City Brisket Rub

1/2 cup paprika
2 tablespoons brown sugar
2 tablespoons chili powder
2 tablespoons onion powder

2 tablespoons kosher salt
2 tablespoons black pepper
1 tablespoon dry mustard
1 1/2 teaspoons red pepper

Makes about 3/4 cup rub

Basic Barbecue Sauce

While bottles of barbecue sauce are available at the supermarket, there's nothing like homemade barbecue sauce to get your salivary glands pumping. You can tinker with the basic recipe by adding a dash of honey, red wine, beef stock, brown sugar, fresh lemon or lime juice, or instant coffee.

4 cups ketchup	1/2 cup molasses, sorghum
4 cups white vinegar	6 tablespoons salt
4 cups water	6 tablespoons black pepper
1 large yellow onion, diced	6 teaspoons chili powder

1. Place all ingredients in a large saucepan and mix well. Bring to a rolling boil; reduce heat and simmer for 1 1/2 hours, stirring every 10 minutes or so.
2. Pour into sterilized jars, seal, and refrigerate 2 to 6 weeks before using.

Makes about 3/4 gallon sauce—great for large events; reduce quantities by 50 percent for smaller yield

Beyond-Belief Barbecue Sauce

Bottled barbecue sauces come in tons of flavors and cost as little as a $1. But once you've experienced the aroma of homemade sauce simmering on the stove, you'll be off your rocker if you buy off the shelf again. This sauce will keep a week or so in the fridge and several months in the freezer if stored in an airtight container.

1 small yellow onion, finely chopped	2 tablespoons brown sugar
1 garlic clove, finely chopped	2 tablespoons Worcestershire sauce
1/2 cup (1 stick) butter or margarine	1 tablespoon freshly squeezed lemon juice
3 tablespoons vinegar	1/2 tablespoon prepared mustard
1 cup bottled chili sauce	1 can beer, any brand
1 cup water	Black pepper to taste

1. In a large saucepan, sauté the onion and garlic in the butter or margarine.
2. When the onions are translucent, add all the remaining ingredients. Bring to a boil and simmer until the barbecue grill is hot, about 10 to 15 minutes. Brush liberally on beef, ribs, or chicken.

Makes about 1 quart sauce

Wet Marinade for Beef

1 cup bourbon, any brand	1/2 cup freshly squeezed lemon juice
1 cup packed light brown sugar	1 tablespoon Worcestershire sauce
2/3 cup soy sauce	2 cups water
1 teaspoon chopped fresh cilantro, or	3 teaspoons chopped fresh thyme, or
1/2 teaspoon ground coriander	1 1/2 teaspoons dried

In a bowl, mix all the ingredients together. Brush liberally on meat. Marinate meat in refrigerator overnight (8 to 12 hours), rotating occasionally.

Makes about 1 quart marinade

Super Citrus Barbecue Sauce

Ancho is a sweet-to-moderately-hot chili pepper often used in Mexican cuisine. Similar in shape to bell peppers, it is brownish black and has a wrinkled skin. You can usually find fresh ancho chilis in gourmet supermarkets (like Wegmans) and Hispanic grocery stores. Or you can buy them (and virtually any type of chili) over the Internet.

1 ancho chili, seeded and finely chopped
1 large yellow onion, finely chopped
1 tablespoon oil, olive or canola
1 tablespoon ground red chili pepper
1/4 teaspoon ground red pepper
1 cup freshly squeezed orange juice
1/2 cup freshly squeezed lime juice
2 tablespoons freshly squeezed lemon juice
2 tablespoons sugar
1 tablespoon finely chopped fresh cilantro
1 teaspoon salt

In a skillet, sauté ancho chili and onion in oil, stirring frequently, about 5 minutes, until onion is translucent and tender. Stir in all remaining ingredients. Heat to boiling; reduce heat to low. Simmer uncovered for about 10 minutes, stirring occasionally.
Makes about 2 1/3 cups sauce.

Georgia Barbecue Sauce

Use sparingly as a basting sauce for fresh pork, ham, ribs, or chicken. Heat additional sauce and serve on the side. The last time I made this, I didn't have cider vinegar, so I used malt vinegar instead.

1/2 cup ketchup
1/3 cup apple cider vinegar
2 tablespoons oil, olive or canola
2 tablespoons Worcestershire sauce
1/2 cup firmly packed light brown sugar

1 tablespoon prepared mustard, brown or yellow
2 to 3 garlic cloves, crushed
1 lemon, halved and seeded

In a small saucepan, combine ketchup, vinegar, oil, Worcestershire sauce, brown sugar, mustard, and garlic. Squeeze juice from lemon into sauce, add shell from 1 lemon half. Cook over medium-low heat for about 10 minutes. Sauce does not need to boil, but heating blends the flavors nicely. Remove lemon shell before using.
Makes about 1 1/2 cups sauce

2
Here's the Beef

Despite its boring reputation, the hamburger is one of the most versatile things you can cook on a grill, and this chapter includes enough burger recipes to satisfy any palate for months. I hope you will enjoy these decidedly different hamburger meals and gain enough confidence to invent your own spice combinations. You can also experiment using ground turkey, ground chicken, or ground pork instead of ground beef. If you hit on a winner, you can name the burger after yourself, like my buddies did.

> **Big Daddy Lowdown:** Raw ground beef can contain harmful bacteria that can make you overly familiar with the inside of your toilet bowl. To reduce your risk for foodborne illness, don't use the same spatula on raw and cooked hamburger patties.

Burgers, Scandinavian Style

1 pound ground beef, regular or lean	1/4 teaspoon garlic powder
1/4 cup ketchup	1/2 cup red wine vinegar
1 tablespoon dried onion flakes	1/4 cup oil, olive or canola
2 teaspoons salt	1/2 teaspoon dried dill weed
1 teaspoon black pepper	2 medium red onions, thinly sliced
1 teaspoon celery seed	1 loaf rye bread or 8 rye buns

1. In a large bowl, combine the meat, ketchup, onion flakes, salt, pepper, celery seed, and garlic powder. Shape the mixture into 16 thin patties; cover and put in fridge.
2. In a small bowl, mix vinegar, oil, and dill. Place the onion slices in a shallow glass dish; pour the vinegar mixture over onions. Cover and marinate in the refrigerator for at least 30 minutes.
3. Wrap the bread or buns in a single thickness in heavy-duty aluminum foil. Place on grill 4 inches from medium coals. Heat 20 minutes, turning occasionally.
4. Remove onions from marinade; reserve marinade. Place hamburgers on grill 4 inches from medium coals. Cook for 5 minutes on each side, or until done, brushing frequently with reserved marinade. Serve 1 hamburger patty per slice of warm bread or roll; top with onions.
Serves 8

Uncle Teddy's Grilled Hamburger Supreme

Like my Uncle Teddy always says, use a meat thermometer to make sure you kill anything in the meat that might otherwise kill your friends (that's 180°F). Actually, Uncle Teddy doesn't say much these days, but that's just because Aunt Marcella has him beaten down. And truth be told, Teddy wasn't the brightest bulb to begin with, so the chances of him having ever spouted any pearls of food safety wisdom are pretty slim. Still, the man cooked a mean burger, and *I'm* here telling you that stuffed friends are better than dead friends, unless you've got a taxidermist in the family.

1 can (3 ounces) mushrooms or
   6 fresh, white button mushrooms,
   chopped
1/4 cup (1/2 stick) butter
1 pound ground round
1/2 teaspoon salt
1/2 teaspoon white pepper
1/2 teaspoon garlic powder
3 tablespoons garlic sauce
   (Cajun Power or other brand)

1 tablespoon Worcestershire sauce
1/2 teaspoon black pepper
4 tablespoons Italian bread crumbs
1 teaspoon Old Bay seasoning
1/2 teaspoon onion powder
1 tomato, sliced
4 slices sharp Cheddar cheese
Lettuce (optional)
Red onion slices (optional)
Onion rolls, halved

1. Sauté mushrooms in butter; set aside.
2. In a large bowl, mix the ground beef with spices thoroughly. Fashion into thin patties—1/4 inch thick and 5 inches in diameter—as they will plump up after grilling.
3. Grill until desired doneness. Garnish with reserved mushrooms, the tomatoes, cheese, lettuce, and red onion slice, if desired. Serve on onion roll.
   Serves 4

Best-of-the-Border Barbecue Brisket

Pit roasting is cooking meat in a large, level hole dug in the earth. A hardwood fire is built in the pit, requiring wood equal to about two and one half times the volume of the pit. The hardwood is allowed to burn until the wood reduces and the pit is half-filled with burning coals. This can require four to six hours of burning time.

3/4 cup salt	9- to 10-pound beef brisket
1/2 cup black pepper	1/4 to 1/3 cup full-flavored beer
1/3 cup chili powder	Barbecue sauce, bottled or homemade
4 1/2 teaspoons cayenne pepper	(see Chapter 1), any flavor

1. Preheat barbecue pit to 250°F. Insert grill rack when wood is sufficiently reduced.
2. Place the salt, black pepper, chili powder, and cayenne pepper into a small bowl and mix well to create dry rub.
3. Cut off fat wedge near large end of brisket, and rub spice mixture onto all sides of the meat. Place any leftover rub on top.
4. Place brisket on grill rack, fat side up, and cook at 250°F to 275°F for 4 hours. Remove meat from pit.
5. Use aluminum foil bag, or make one large enough from heavy-duty foil to hold brisket, leaving one side open. Put meat in bag and add beer. Tightly seal all edges of foil.
6. Return bagged brisket to pit. Raise temperature to 300°F. Let pit cook back down to 225°F to 250°F degrees and cook 3 hours more.
7. Remove brisket from pit, and top with favorite barbecue sauce. Slice and serve.
   Serves your company softball team (about 20 people)

Chili Barbecued Beef

Cooking the spices, even for a few seconds, helps reduce their rawness. I bet my wife that she couldn't guess the ingredients in the marinade—it tastes sweeter than you might expect. She lost. I won—a victory sweeter than you might expect!

4 teaspoons ground cumin
2 teaspoons chili powder
1/8 teaspoon ground cinnamon
1/4 cup olive oil
1/4 cup freshly squeezed lime juice
1/4 cup balsamic vinegar
2 tablespoons molasses

2 tablespoons chopped fresh
   oregano, or 1 teaspoon dried
1 tablespoon minced garlic
1/2 to 1 1/2 pounds beef flank,
   top round steak, or pork tender
Curly endive, radishes, or other
   greens (for garnish)

1. Make the marinade by combining cumin, chili powder, and cinnamon in a small saucepan. Cook and mix over high heat about 40 seconds until fragrant. Whisk in oil, lime juice, vinegar, molasses, oregano, and garlic.
2. Pour marinade over meat in a shallow dish, turning to coat. Cover and marinate in the refrigerator for 4 hours or overnight.
3. Remove meat from refrigerator 30 minutes before grilling. Prepare grill. Remove meat from marinade. Grill beef over medium coals, basting occasionally, 7 to 8 minutes per side for medium-rare (12 to 15 minutes if using pork), until meat thermometer inserted into thickest part reaches 160°F. Let stand 5 minutes. Slice thin across the grain. Serve with a black-bean salsa (found in the Mexican-food section of most grocery stores).

Serves 1 to 2, depending on how hungry you are

Shredded Barbecued Beef Sandwiches

Curious about Colgin's Liquid Smoke, I checked out the manufacturer's Web site and was surprised to learn that this cooking sauce can actually reduce harmful strains of E. coli bacteria from meat. The sauce is made by burning hickory, mesquite, apple, and pecan wood chips at very high temperatures and moisture levels. The gasses produced are quickly chilled in condensers, which liquifies the smoke. The liquid is then refined and aged in oak barrels.

6 pounds beef brisket
1/2 teaspoon Colgin's Liquid Smoke
1 teaspoon salt
1/2 teaspoon paprika

1/2 teaspoon garlic powder
1/2 teaspoon dry mustard
10 French or other long or round
   crusty rolls

BARBECUE SAUCE:
2 tablespoons canola oil
1/2 cup chopped Vidalia onions
2 tablespoons minced garlic
1/2 teaspoon ground cumin
1/4 teaspoon cayenne pepper

1 cup ketchup
1/2 cup malt vinegar
1/4 cup packed dark brown sugar
2 tablespoons Worcestershire sauce
1/2 teaspoon Colgin's Liquid Smoke

1. Barbecue sauce: Heat oil in a medium-size pan. Add the onion, garlic, cumin, and cayenne and sauté over medium-high heat for 5 minutes or until the onions are light brown.
2. Stir in the remaining ingredients. Simmer and stir about 10 minutes, until slightly thickened. (Makes 2 cups.)
3. Brisket: Preheat oven to 350°F.
4. Place brisket in a roasting pan and brush with liquid smoke. Combine salt and spices in a small bowl, mixing well. Brush salt-spice mix on to brisket.

5. Cover roasting pan and bake about 3 hours until brisket is fork tender. Remove pan from oven, and use two forks to pull the meat apart, shredding it coarsely.

6. For each sandwich, halve a roll. Put 2 tablespoons of heated barbecue sauce on the roll, and using a slotted spoon, pile about 1 cup of the shredded meat on top of the sauce. Pour another 2 to 3 tablespoons of sauce over the meat, and cover with the top half of roll. Serve with additional barbecue sauce on the side.
    Serves 10

Barbecue Meat Loaf "Aussie" Style

Refrigerate leftovers—you can slap a slab on a bun for a hearty lunch. The sauce tastes awesome on ribs or chicken, too, so consider making a double batch and freezing some in an airtight container.

LOAF:

Nonstick cooking spray
1 pound lean ground beef
1 pound sausage, casing removed
1 cup fine bread crumbs
2 medium yellow onions, finely chopped
Salt and pepper to taste
1 tablespoon curry powder

1 tablespoon chopped fresh parsley, or 1 teaspoon dried
1 garlic clove, crushed
1 large egg, beaten
1/2 cup milk, whole, 2%, or fat-free—whatever's in the fridge
1/2 cup water

BARBECUE SAUCE:

1 medium yellow onion, finely chopped
2 tablespoons margarine
1/4 cup water
1/2 cup ketchup
1/4 cup dry red wine or beef stock

1/4 cup Worcestershire sauce (I like Lea & Perrins, but any brand will do the trick)
2 tablespoons vinegar
1 tablespoon instant coffee powder
1/4 cup packed light brown sugar
2 teaspoons lemon juice, fresh or bottled

1. Preheat oven to 375°F. Spray an ovenproof loaf pan with nonstick cooking spray.
2. In a large bowl, combine beef, sausage, bread crumbs, onions, salt, pepper, curry powder, parsley, garlic, and egg, mixing well.
3. Mix milk and water, then add to meat mixture a little at a time until texture is smooth but firm. Shape into

a loaf and put into prepared pan. Bake for 30 minutes.
4. In a sauté pan, cook onions in margarine until golden. Add remaining sauce ingredients to pan. Bring slowly to a boil, lower heat, and simmer for 10 to 15 minutes.
5. After the loaf has cooked for 30 minutes, pour half of the sauce over the meat, return to oven, and bake 45 minutes more, basting often with remaining sauce. Serve loaf hot in thick slices with remaining sauce.
Serves 8

River City Rub's Brisket

Here's the first of several from the River City boys . . . enjoy!

1/2 cup soy sauce
1/2 cup Worcestershire sauce
7- to 8-pound brisket flat

1 cup of River City Brisket Rub recipe
  (see page 20)
Olive oil

1. In a small bowl, mix the soy sauce and Worcestershire sauce together and spread evenly over the flat. Then lay down an even coat of olive oil and sprinkle rub over the meat, coating both sides.
2. Get smoker to an internal temperature of 225°F. Place meat on smoker and add wood immediately. (Be careful not to use too much wood when cooking a brisket. It doesn't require a lot a wood to get a good smoked flavor. Two to three chunks of your favorite wood will be more than enough.) Cook meat for about 1 1/2 hours per pound.
3. After about 7 hours, or when meat reaches about 160°F, wrap in foil. Cook for the remaining allotted time until the internal temperature reaches 195°F.
4. Slice brisket in 1/4-inch pieces across the grain and serve with or without barbecue sauce.
Serves 10 to 12

3

Best Barbecued Beef Steaks

If you're satisfied eating steak or chicken barbecued straight up, you obviously haven't discovered the magic of marinating. Marinating meat and poultry for several hours to a couple of days before cooking adds both flavor and tenderness. Bluntly stated, most barbecue connoisseurs wouldn't be caught dead cooking or eating beef that has not been bathed in marinade.

Although marinating takes a bit of advanced planning, it's really a snap; you basically mix the marinade ingredients together, pour it over your meat in one of those zip-seal plastic bags, toss the bag into the fridge, then go shoot some hoops, catch a movie, have sex, and go to sleep.

Big Daddy Lowdown: Always marinate in the refrigerator, not at room temperature. If some of the marinade is to be used as a sauce on the cooked food, reserve a portion of the marinade before putting raw meat and poultry in it. However, if the marinade that was used on raw meat or poultry is to be reused, boil the marinade first to destroy any harmful bacteria.

Frank's Flank Steaks

Frank is my wife's sister's brother-in-law, and no, I'm not talking about myself. Anyway, we busted his . . . chops . . . for years, because as hard as the boy tried, he managed to mangle every cut of meat he came across. The thing is, he was trying too hard, trying to be fancy without really knowing what he was doing. Anyway, one Fourth of July he brought out a tray of these flanks, and I was so impressed I asked him for the recipe. He told me that if I wanted it that bad, I'd have to put it in my book. I did, and here it is—simple, but worth it.

2 tablespoons dry mustard	2 tablespoons olive oil
1/2 teaspoon salt	1 garlic clove, chopped
1/4 teaspoon black pepper	1/3 cup freshly squeezed lemon juice
1/4 cup packed light brown sugar	Meat tenderizer (like Adolph's)
2 tablespoons soy sauce	2 large flank steaks

1. In a medium bowl, whisk together the first 8 ingredients (mustard through lemon juice) to make basting sauce; set aside.
2. Sprinkle meat tenderizer onto flank steaks and put steaks into a shallow pan.
3. Generously pour sauce over steaks. Cover and marinate in the refrigerator for at least 2 hours.
4. Remove steaks from basting sauce and grill over medium heat for about 3 to 5 minutes per side. Baste with additional sauce, if desired.

Serves 6

Beer-Barbecued Flank Steaks

2 cans (14 1/2 ounces each) beef
    stock (consommé)
2/3 cup soy sauce
1/2 cup chopped scallions (green onion)
6 tablespoons freshly squeezed
    lime juice

4 tablespoons packed light
    brown sugar
1 garlic clove, crushed
2 large flank steaks
2 cups full-flavor beer

1. In a large bowl, combine first 6 ingredients (beef stock through garlic), and pour over steaks in a dish. Pour in the beer. Marinate in the refrigerator for 24 hours.
2. Barbecue over medium heat until done to your liking. Slice thin across the grain and serve.
    Serves 8

Charbroiled Rib-Eye Steaks

A hinged-wire hand grill basket is a great tool for barbecuing veggies, as this recipe calls for, as well as whole fish and sandwiches. Be sure to oil the hinged grill before adding food and placing it on the barbecue rack.

1/2 cup (1 stick) butter, melted	2 green bell peppers, sliced thin
1 lemon, halved	2 white onions, sliced thin
Tabasco or other hot sauce to taste	2 tomatoes, sliced
1 pound mushrooms, sliced	6 rib-eye steaks, 1 inch thick

1. In a small bowl, combine the butter, juice from both lemon halves, grated peel of one lemon half, and a dash or more of hot sauce. Put 1/3 to 1/4 of the sauce into a separate container. Refrigerate.
2. Place the mushrooms, peppers, onions, and tomatoes into a hinged-wire grill and close to hold them in place. Place on grill over medium-high heat. Using the larger portion of the lemon sauce, baste and turn vegetables frequently. When the vegetables start to sizzle and soften, move to the coolest area of grill surface.
3. On the hottest part of the grill, cook steaks for 5 minutes about 2 inches from heat source. Baste with lemon sauce and turn over every minute or so, basting frequently. Grill 5 minutes more for rare (total 10 minutes), 10 minutes for medium (total 15 minutes), or 15 minutes for well done (total 20 minutes).
4. Transfer steaks to serving platter and dump vegetables over them. Gently heat reserved sauce and pour sauce over vegetables.
Serves 6

Herbed Steak and Onions

1 cup canned tomato juice
1 tablespoon olive oil or other
  cooking oil
1/2 teaspoon dried basil, crushed
1/2 teaspoon dried oregano, crushed
1/4 teaspoon black pepper

1 garlic clove, minced
1 pound top round steak, 1 inch thick
2 large yellow or white onions,
  sliced thin and separated into
  rings
Nonstick cooking spray

1. In a small bowl, combine the tomato juice, oil, basil, oregano, pepper, and garlic to create marinade; set aside.
2. Trim fat from steak and cut into four equal portions. Place meat in a zip-seal bag set in a deep bowl. Pour marinade over steak. Seal bag; turn to coat steak well. Marinate in the refrigerator overnight.
3. Drain steak, reserving marinade. Spray an 18-inch square of foil with cooking spray. Place onion slices on foil and turn up edges of foil slightly.
4. Pour about 1/2 cup of the reserved marinade into a saucepan and bring to a boil, then drizzle over onions. Fold foil tightly to seal.
5. Grill onion packet and steak on uncovered grill over medium heat for 10 minutes. Turn onion packet and steak; brush steak with marinade. Grill steak to desired doneness (5 minutes more for rare, 10 minutes for medium, 15 minutes for well done). Grill onions another 8 minutes more or until tender.
6. Unwrap onions and place on serving plate. Arrange meat atop onions. Spoon any remaining sauce from onions over the meat.

Serves 4

Uncle Jack's Grilled Chuck Roast

Uncle Jack isn't so much a relative as he is a family institution. Cooking with Jack Daniel's whiskey is a tradition at my house, so is drinking it for that matter, but for these next two recipes, both calling for whiskey (and don't we all from time to time), you can use any bottle you're willing to sacrifice.

1/3 cup Jack Daniel's whiskey
1/2 cup packed light brown sugar
1/3 cup soy sauce
1/3 cup water
1 tablespoon Worcestershire sauce

1 teaspoon freshly squeezed
  lemon juice
1/8 teaspoon garlic powder
2 1/2 pounds chuck roast

1. In a medium bowl, combine the whiskey, brown sugar, soy sauce, water, Worcestershire sauce, lemon juice, and garlic powder, mixing well.
2. Place roast into a large zip-seal bag; add marinade and seal. Place in a shallow dish and marinate in the refrigerator for 8 hours or overnight, turning occasionally.
3. Remove roast from bag and grill over medium heat (with water-soaked Jack Daniel's Barrel Chips, if you can find them), about 20 to 25 minutes per side for medium, basting occasionally with marinade.
4. To serve, cut into thin slices.
   Serves 4 to 6

Old No. 7 Flank Steak

1 1/2 pounds flank steak, 1/2 inch
   thick
1 garlic clove, minced
2 teaspoons dry mustard

1/4 cup Jack Daniel's whiskey
2 tablespoons butter or margarine
Salt and black pepper to taste

1. Score flank steak with a sharp knife, about 1/8 inch deep, in a diamond pattern; set aside. Mash garlic into dry mustard; stir in whiskey. Put steak in large zip-seal bag; pour mixture over steak, seal bag, place in a shallow dish, and refrigerate overnight.
2. Using a charcoal or gas grill, cook over high heat, 3 to 5 minutes per side, dotting each side with butter or margarine while cooking. When done, transfer steak to cutting board and slice immediately by cutting across the grain into 1/4-inch-thick slices. Sprinkle with salt and pepper.

Serves 4

Peppered Rib-Eye Steaks

4 beef rib-eye steaks, 1 1/2 inches
    thick
1 tablespoon olive oil
1 tablespoon garlic powder
1 tablespoon paprika
2 teaspoons dried thyme
2 teaspoons dried oregano

1 1/2 teaspoons black pepper
1 teaspoon salt
1 teaspoon lemon pepper
1 teaspoon ground red pepper
Orange slices (optional)
Parsley sprigs (optional)

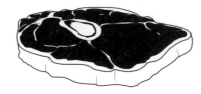

1. Brush steaks lightly with olive oil. In a small bowl, combine the next 8 ingredients (garlic powder through red pepper). Sprinkle seasoning blend over steaks and press into both sides. Cover and refrigerate for 1 hour.
2. Grill steaks, turning once, over medium-hot coals—14 to 18 minutes for rare, 18 to 22 minutes for medium, 24 to 38 minutes for well done. Place on cutting board or serving platter; cut across the grain into thick slices. Garnish with orange slices and parsley, if desired.
Serves 8

Smoked Prime Rib

4 teaspoons paprika
2 teaspoons salt
2 teaspoons onion powder
2 teaspoons ground black pepper

1 teaspoon cayenne pepper
8-pound prime-rib roast
Dried rosemary, crushed

1. In a small bowl, combine the first 5 ingredients (paprika through cayenne); rub over entire roast surface. Let stand until rub appears wet.
2. Grill roast in smoker (indirect heat) for 3 to 4 hours at 200°F to 250°F, or until a meat thermometer indicates an internal temperature of at least 140°F (for medium rare). About an hour before the roast is done, sprinkle crushed rosemary leaves onto meat.

Serves 8

Steak Teriyaki

1/2 cup soy sauce
3 tablespoons packed brown sugar
1 teaspoon ground ginger
1/2 teaspoon dry mustard
1/2 teaspoon coarsely ground
   black pepper
1/4 teaspoon garlic powder

2 tablespoons freshly squeezed
   lemon juice
1 can (12 ounces) beer, flat, any
   brand
2 tablespoons oil, olive or canola
3 pounds round or sirloin steaks,
   1 inch thick

1. Combine the marinade ingredients (soy sauce through oil) and pour over steak in large zip-seal bag or covered dish. Marinate in the refrigerator for 12 to 24 hours.
2. Grill 3 to 4 inches from hot coals, basting frequently with marinade, for about 10 minutes per side, or to desired doneness. Slice steak thin on the diagonal and serve.

Serves 3 to 4

Teriyaki Flank Steak

Any steak may be substituted for flank.

1 1/2 pounds flank steak
1/4 cup pineapple juice
1/4 cup soy sauce
2 tablespoons oil, olive or canola
1 teaspoon ground ginger

2 tablespoons cider vinegar
1 tablespoon honey
1 garlic clove
2 tablespoons chopped yellow onion

1. Trim excess fat from steak; place steak in a shallow dish or large zip-seal bag.
2. Combine the next 7 ingredients (pineapple juice through garlic), stirring well. Pour marinade over steak. Cover dish or seal bag and marinate in the refrigerator for 8 hours or overnight.
3. Remove steak and reserve marinade. Grill steak 5 inches from hot coals 5 to 7 minutes per side or until desired doneness. Baste with marinade during cooking. Garnish with chopped onion.

Serves 6

4
You're Ribbin' Me

Take it from Big Daddy: The best way to cook ribs is by smoking them. Smoking means cooking food indirectly in the presence of a fire. It can be done in a covered grill if a pan of water is placed beneath the meat as it sizzles. You can also cook ribs in an outdoor cooker called a smoker, which is especially designed for smoking foods.

Because smoking is done much more slowly than grilling, meats that are less tender benefit greatly from this method, which permeates the meat with a natural smoke flavoring.

> **Big Daddy Lowdown:** The temperature in the smoker should be maintained at 250°F to 300°F for optimal safety, although some recipes will call for a slightly lower temperature.

General Rib-Smoking Directions

1. Season or marinate meat according to recipe.
2. Prepare smoker for long, slow cooking using hickory chips for flavor. Cook ribs, bone side down, at 230°F for 2 hours using indirect heat. Turn and cook 1 hour more.
3. Mix 2 parts barbecue sauce with 1 part water. During the final 15 minutes of cooking time, baste the ribs with diluted barbecue sauce. Serve ribs with warm, undiluted sauce on the side.

Barbecue Rum Ribs

4 pounds spareribs
1/4 cup ketchup
1 teaspoon dry mustard
1/4 cup dark rum, any brand
2 garlic cloves, crushed

1 cup packed light brown sugar
1/4 cup soy sauce
1/2 cup bottled chili sauce
1/4 cup Worcestershire sauce
Dash black pepper

1. Wrap ribs in double thickness of foil and bake at 350°F for 1 1/2 hours. Unwrap and drain drippings.
2. Combine remaining ingredients (ketchup through black pepper), and pour over ribs. Marinate at room temperature for 1 hour. Bake at 350°F for 30 minutes, basting occasionally with sauce.

Serves 4

Baby's Big Daddy Loves Short Ribs

Short ribs can be ordered from retailers. They are cut 3/8 to 1/2 inch thick. Each has three crosscut rib bones.

4 pounds beef short ribs
1 teaspoon salt (optional)
3/4 cup chopped onion
1 tablespoon salad oil
3/4 cup ketchup
1/2 cup maple syrup, regular
  or low-calorie

1/3 cup freshly squeezed lemon juice
3 tablespoons Worcestershire sauce
2 tablespoons prepared mustard,
  brown or yellow
1/4 teaspoon black pepper

1. Trim excess fat from ribs. Place ribs and salt in a 4-quart saucepan or Dutch oven. Cover with water. Bring to a boil; lower heat, cover, and simmer for 1 1/2 to 2 hours, until tender.
2. Meanwhile, in a skillet, sauté the onion in oil until tender. Add remaining ingredients (ketchup through black pepper); simmer 15 minutes.
3. Drain ribs. Place on rack in broiler pan or over ash-colored coals on outdoor grill so meat is 6 to 7 inches from heat. Broil for 10 minutes, turning occasionally. Baste ribs with sauce; continue broiling 10 minutes more, turning and basting frequently with sauce. Serve with remaining sauce, if desired.

Serves 6

Barbecued Chili Pork Spareribs

2 racks pork spareribs	3 tablespoons packed light brown sugar
8 dried red chili peppers, seeded	2 teaspoons salt
3/4 cup hot water	3 tablespoons tequila, any brand
1/2 cup ketchup	1/2 cup oil, olive or canola
2 garlic cloves, peeled	1/2 teaspoon ground cumin
1/2 cup cider vinegar	1/8 teaspoon ground allspice

1. In a large kettle, cover the spareribs with water; bring to boil and simmer the ribs, skimming the froth as necessary, for about 50 minutes. Drain ribs well and pat dry.
2. While ribs are simmering, place the remaining ingredients (chili peppers through allspice) in a blender and purée.
3. On a jelly-roll pan or tray, coat the ribs generously with chili sauce, reserving the remaining sauce in a small bowl. Cover ribs with plastic wrap and refrigerate ribs and leftover sauce for at least 8 hours or overnight.
4. Let ribs stand at room temperature for 1 hour; grill them on an oiled rack set 5 to 6 inches above heat source for 6 minutes per side.
5. In a small saucepan, simmer the reserved chili sauce for 3 minutes. Serve with the ribs.
   Serves 6

Mooney's Sticky Monster Bones

> **Big Daddy Lowdown:** Uncooked ribs can be frozen in the marinade in a zip-seal bag. Refrigerate for 24 hours before grilling. After fully cooked, these ribs will hold nicely in the oven (200°F) if covered.

1 cup mesquite-flavored
  barbecue sauce
1/4 cup apple cider
5 pounds meaty beef ribs
1 can (10 1/2 ounces) beef broth

4 tablespoons dry-rub seasoning
  (see Chapter 1)
Barbecue sauce, bottled or
  homemade (see Chapter 1)

1. In a small bowl, combine the mesquite-flavored barbecue sauce and apple cider to create marinade. Place the ribs in a shallow dish; pour marinade over ribs and refrigerate overnight.
2. Set up grill using chunks of hickory wood. Pour beef broth into the drip pan; sprinkle in about 2 tablespoons of dry-rub seasoning.
3. Remove ribs from marinade and drain. Sprinkle liberally with dry-rub seasoning. Place ribs on grill over the drip pan and smoke for 2 1/2 to 3 hours. Brush with barbecue sauce two or three times during the final hour. Serve with extra sauce.

Serves 2 to 3

New Mexico Barbecue Beef Ribs

Searing meat on a hot barbecue grill is the best way to lock in the juices. Be careful, though; the surface of the meat cooks and crisps up quickly. Soon as that happens, remove the ribs from the grill before they burn.

1/3 cup bottled chili sauce
1 cup dry red wine
2 tablespoons olive oil
1 garlic clove, large (or 2 small), minced

1 medium yellow onion, diced
1/2 teaspoon salt
1/4 teaspoon freshly ground black pepper
4 pounds beef short ribs

1. In a large bowl, combine all the ingredients except ribs. Let mixture stand at room temperature for 15 minutes.
2. Marinate ribs in sauce thoroughly. Sear 5 minutes per side. Cover grill with heavy aluminum foil; add ribs, and spoon sauce over them. Cook for 5 minutes, turn and spoon more sauce. Continue turning and saucing every 15 to 30 minutes until done.
Serves 1 to 2

Oriental Short Rib Barbecue

Raw sesame seeds are sold in the spice section of the supermarket. To toast, put seeds in dry sauté pan and heat over a medium flame while mixing the seeds around constantly with a wooden spoon. It takes about a minute for the seeds to turn golden brown, but only a few seconds longer for them to burn to a crisp! Let them cool before crushing them on a cutting board using the back of a spoon.

2/3 cup thinly sliced green onions
1 1/2 tablespoons toasted sesame seeds, crushed
1 cup soy sauce
1 cup water
1 tablespoon minced fresh garlic
1 tablespoon grated fresh ginger
1/4 cup dark sesame oil

2 1/2 tablespoons packed light brown sugar
1/2 teaspoon red pepper
1/8 teaspoon red pepper pods, crushed
4 pounds beef short ribs, well trimmed

1. In a medium bowl, combine all the ingredients except ribs. Put 2 to 3 tablespoons of the marinade in a small container and refrigerate.
2. Place short ribs in a large zip-seal bag; add the rest of the marinade, turning to coat. Close bag securely and marinate in the refrigerator for 4 to 6 hours (or overnight, if desired), turning occasionally.
3. Remove ribs from marinade. Place ribs on grill over medium coals; cover. Grill 10 to 12 minutes, turning once and brushing with reserved marinade.
    Serves 12

Rattlesnake Ribs

Don't be intimidated by the quantity of ingredients listed below; the braising liquid, spice mixture, and sauce use many of the same items. One of America's finest chefs, Jimmy Schmidt of the Rattlesnake Club in Denver, has made Rattlesnake Ribs a signature dish. Salsas come in varying degrees of hotness. For the sauce in this dish, Big Daddy recommends one that packs a substantial wallop. The three sauces create a deep, hot flavor—these are real mean western ribs.

4 slabs baby back ribs (about 1 1/4 pounds each)

BARBECUE SAUCE:
1 cup bottled chili sauce
1 cup ketchup
1/4 cup steak sauce (any brand)
1 tablespoon Worcestershire sauce
1 tablespoon minced garlic
1/4 cup finely grated fresh
  horseradish; or 2 tablespoons
  prepared, well drained

3 tablespoons dry mustard
1 tablespoon Tabasco sauce
1 tablespoon molasses
1 tablespoon salsa
1 tablespoon red wine vinegar

BRAISING LIQUID:
4 quarts beef stock, homemade or
  canned
3/4 cup red wine vinegar
1 tablespoon paprika
1 tablespoon cayenne pepper
1 1/2 tablespoons ground cumin

3 tablespoons Tabasco sauce
1 1/4 tablespoons garlic powder
1 tablespoon ground ginger
1 cup tomato paste
1/4 cup honey
1 tablespoon salt

SPICE PASTE:

1/4 cup garlic salt	1/4 cup red wine vinegar
1 tablespoon ground white pepper	1/4 cup Worcestershire sauce
1/2 cup paprika	1/2 cup beer, any brand
1/4 cup dry mustard	

1. In a medium-size bowl, combine all the barbecue sauce ingredients (chili through red wine vinegar) and whisk until the sauce is well blended. Adjust seasonings to taste and refrigerate in airtight container until needed. (Makes 3 cups.)

2. In a large pot, combine all the braising liquid ingredients (beef stock through salt). Stir well and bring to a simmer over medium heat.

3. Add the ribs and simmer until tender but not falling apart, about 1 hour and 45 minutes. When done, carefully transfer ribs to a baking sheet.

4. In a medium-size bowl, combine all the spice paste ingredients (salt through beer) and stir to form a paste (add more beer if it's too dry). Rub the spice paste over all surfaces of the ribs.

5. Wrap each slab in aluminum foil, dull side out, and refrigerate until ready to cook. (These can be prepared up to 4 days in advance.)

6. Preheat oven to 400°F, and heat coals for grilling. Place the rack of ribs on the grill, 3 to 4 inches from the coals, for about 30 minutes, turning frequently.

7. Transfer the ribs from the grill to a baking sheet covered with aluminum foil. Coat the ribs with 2 cups of the barbecue sauce, and bake on the center rack of the oven for 10 minutes.

8. Transfer the ribs back to grill, and cook just long enough to char. Serve immediately with the remaining cup of barbecue sauce on the side.

Serves 4

Championship Barbecued Ribs

5 pounds pork-loin back ribs

BARBECUE SAUCE:
6 tablespoons salt
6 tablespoons black pepper
6 tablespoons chili powder
4 cups ketchup

4 cups white vinegar
4 cups water
1 large yellow onion, diced
1/2 cup molasses, sorghum

DRY RUB:
4 tablespoons paprika
2 teaspoons salt
2 teaspoons onion powder

2 teaspoons black pepper
2 teaspoons white pepper
2 teaspoons ground red pepper

1. In a large saucepan, combine barbecue sauce ingredients (salt through molasses). Bring to a rolling boil; reduce heat and simmer for 1 1/2 hours, stirring every 10 minutes or so. Pour into sterilized canning jars, seal, and let stand 2 to 6 weeks before use. (If you can stand to wait, that is. You can use it sooner, but like a fine wine, it won't taste as good.)
2. In a small bowl, mix all dry rub ingredients (paprika through red pepper) together thoroughly. Sprinkle dry rub liberally onto ribs. Allow ribs to stand for 20 to 30 minutes at room temperature until the rub appears wet.
3. Prepare smoker for long, slow (230°F) indirect cooking, using hickory chips or other hardwood chips for extra flavor. Cook ribs, bone side down, for 2 hours at 230°F in a smoker using indirect heat. Turn and cook 2 hours more. Turn again, and cook 1 hour more. During the last 15 minutes, baste with barbecue sauce diluted by half with water. Serve ribs warmed with undiluted sauce on the side.
    Serves 1 to 2

River City Rub's Ribs

4 to 6 pounds loin back ribs
1/4 cup prepared mustard
1 cup River City Pork Rub
   (see page 20)

1 cup apple juice (in a spray bottle)
1 cup barbecue sauce
1/4 cup honey

1. Take the ribs and peel the membrane off the back of each slab, then rinse the slab off to get rid of bone dust. Dry with cotton towel and lightly coat the ribs with mustard. Take shaker of rub and lightly coat both sides of meat. Get smoker to a temperature of 220°F (leave damper open so you don't trap stale smoke in chamber). Place ribs in smoker and toss three or four chunks of your favorite wood onto the fire.

Big Daddy Lowdown: Hickory works great here; it gives the ribs a smoky, baconlike flavor. Pecan is also good, similar to hickory, but not as strong.

2. Spray ribs with apple juice once an hour. After about 3 hours, when the meat should be a nice dark color, spray one last time and wrap in foil. Let ribs cook in foil for another 2 hours, giving you a total cook time of 5 hours.
3. Unwrap ribs (carefully), lift them out of the juice, and brush on room-temperature barbecue sauce mixed with honey.
4. Place back in smoker for 15 to 20 minutes unwrapped to allow the meat to draw up.
    Serves 6

Memphis-Style Ribs

These pork ribs are crunchy brown on the outside and lean white in the middle, with a sweet-and-tangy sauce. Below are recipes for the dry marinade, basting sauce, and dipping sauce. Next, you'll find two ways of cooking the ribs—using a smoker and a Weber kettle. Yeah, yeah, I know, the time and planning needed to make this dish can be a pain in the patoot. (You have to marinate the ribs for a day or two before cooking them—for up to 9 hours.) But trust me–it's a small price to pay for the most mouthwatering ribs you'll ever lock a lip on.

SPICY DRY MARINADE:

3 tablespoons mild Hungarian paprika
2 teaspoons seasoned salt
2 teaspoons freshly ground black pepper
2 teaspoons garlic powder
1 teaspoon cayenne pepper
1 teaspoon dried oregano

1 teaspoon dry mustard
1/2 teaspoon chili powder, or more, to taste
1 teaspoon dried thyme
1 teaspoon dried coriander
2 teaspoons dried green peppercorns
1 teaspoon finely ground allspice

Place all ingredients in a food processor and process until mixture is fine and well combined.

BASTING SAUCE:

1/4 cup loosely packed brown sugar
1 1/2 tablespoons spicy dry marinade (see above)
2 cups red wine vinegar

2 cups water
1/4 cup Worcestershire sauce
1/2 teaspoon Tabasco sauce
2 bay leaves

In a medium-size bowl, combine all the ingredients well. Keep basting sauce in an airtight glass bottle or jar and refrigerate until needed.

Big Daddy Lowdown: Baste the ribs with the marinade only during the last half hour of cooking, to glaze the ribs and make them slightly brown. If this sauce is put on the ribs too early, the sugar will blacken the outside of the ribs and be unpleasant looking but not bad tasting. The goal is NOT to blacken the outside of the ribs at all, so I usually serve the sauce at the table near the ribs.

SWEET DIPPING SAUCE:
- 1 can (8 ounces) tomato sauce
- 1/2 cup spicy honey mustard
- 1 cup ketchup
- 1 cup red wine vinegar
- 1 cup water
- 1/4 cup smoked Worcestershire sauce
- 1/4 cup regular Worcestershire sauce
- 1/4 cup oil, olive or canola
- 2 tablespoons Tabasco sauce
- 1 tablespoon freshly squeezed lemon juice
- 2 tablespoons packed brown sugar
- 1 tablespoon mild Hungarian paprika
- 1 tablespoon seasoned salt
- 1 1/2 tablespoons garlic powder, or 5 fresh garlic cloves, minced
- 1/8 teaspoon chili powder
- 1/8 teaspoon cayenne pepper
- 1/8 teaspoon white pepper
- Freshly ground black pepper to taste
- 1/8 teaspoon chili powder
- 1 bay leaf

In a large, heavyweight Dutch oven, combine all the ingredients. Bring to a boil; reduce heat and simmer 30 minutes, stirring occasionally. This sauce should be served at the table with the ribs as a dipping sauce.

Big Daddy Lowdown: Don't baste with this sauce while the ribs are on the grill. Better to paint the sauce on the ribs when they are off the grill but still hot; they will glaze to perfection.

BARBECUING THE RIBS—MEMPHIS STYLE:

8 to 9 pounds pork ribs   Basting sauce (see page 56)

Spicy dry marinade (see page 56)   Sweet dipping sauce (see page 57)

SMOKER METHOD:

1. Wash spareribs in clear water; pat dry. Hand-rub the dry marinade onto the spareribs; cover and refrigerate for 24 to 48 hours.
2. In a smoker, create a low, smoky fire (225°F), using white oak or hickory chips, if possible. Place marinated ribs on a horizontal rack and baste with the basting sauce. Turn and baste every half hour or so. Cooking could take 5 to 9 hours, depending on the size of the cooker and the temperature. Stop using the basting sauce about an hour before serving.
3. Warm the sweet dipping sauce. When ribs are done and hot off the grill, brush on some dipping sauce and serve the rest on the side.

WEBER KETTLE METHOD:

1. Wash spareribs under cold running water; pat dry. Hand-rub the dry marinade onto the spareribs; cover and refrigerate for 24 to 48 hours.
2. Prepare low, indirect fire using chunk-style charcoal. Use a water-filled drip pan under the ribs and a boiling pot of water over the coals. Stand the ribs up on edge in a vertical rack, and try to cook the ribs on a calm day (wind speed under 10 mph). Cook 5 to 7 hours, basting every half hour or so, with the basting sauce. Stop basting about an hour before serving.
3. Warm the sweet dipping sauce. When ribs are done and hot off the grill, brush on some dipping sauce and serve the rest on the side.

Serves 8

Budha's Bone-lickin' Marinade and Ribs

If you could slow-cook innuendo, Budha would win a prize for that too—not that he hasn't already taken home his share. The first year he cooked in the American Royal BBQ he took seventeenth in Ribs with this recipe. In the last four years his team has had six top-three finishes in multiple categories at competitions like the Great Lenexa BBQ Battle and the Great Plains BBQ Cook-off.

Budha starts with whole slabs of ribs and cuts them down "Kansas City" style by removing the brisket, or rib tips, and the skirt. After the ribs are trimmed they resemble baby back ribs. He cooks the tips and skirt separately and either serves them as appetizers or cuts them up for baked beans (See Budha's Musical Fruit). In his own words: "These ribs are so good you will want to lick the bone. And remember, it's good to get a little on ya!"

2 to 3 slabs spare ribs
1 cup Frank's RedHot sauce
1 cup olive oil
2 cups soy sauce
2 cups vinegar
1 1/2 cups maple syrup
1 cup pineapple juice

1 cup apple juice
1 1/2 cups Dijon mustard
2 cups of Budha's All-Purpose Meat
   Rub (see page 17)
1 cup Gates Sweet & Mild BBQ
   Sauce
1 cup honey

1. Remove ribs from packaging and rinse in a vinegar and water bath. Pat the ribs dry with a paper towel. Turn the ribs bone side up and remove the membrane.
2. Once trimmed, roll the ribs and place them in a 2.5-gallon Glad bag. In a medium-size plastic container, combine hot sauce, olive oil, soy sauce, vinegar, 3/4 cup

of maple syrup, pineapple juice, and apple juice. Pour half of the mixture into the bag and seal, removing any extra air, and marinate in the refrigerator for 8 hours (Food Saver vacuum bags can also be used). Refrigerate the other half of the mixture in a separate plastic container and save this to be used later as a baste.

3. Remove the bag from the refrigerator and the ribs from the bag. Rub the ribs with Dijon mustard, then coat with Budha's All-Purpose Rub. Allow the ribs to come up to room temperature while you prepare your smoker.

4. Place the ribs in the smoker and cook at 225°F. After 2 hours, baste the ribs every half hour for the next hour and a half. The ribs will begin to turn a mahogany color.

5. Remove the ribs from the smoker and wrap the slabs individually in aluminum foil.

6. Place 1/2 cup of reserved baste into the foil with each slab. Place the ribs back into the smoker at 225°F for 1 hour. Remove the ribs from the smoker.

7. In a small bowl, combine the barbecue sauce, honey, and 3/4 cup maple syrup to make the glaze. Remove the ribs from foil and slather with glaze. Cook over hot grill for 25 to 45 seconds per side to caramelize. Cut the ribs and serve with glaze on the table.

Serves 4 to 5

5
Don't Be Chicken—Grill It

Welcome to the wonderful world of barbecuing birds. Here you'll find a flock of chicken dishes with a few turkey and duck recipes folded in.

Several recipes tell you to cut a whole chicken into pieces, halves, or quarters. As macho as this may sound, do yourself a favor and buy an already cut-up bird. Cutting up raw chicken is messy, slippery, and about as much fun as unclogging a kitchen sink.

Big Daddy Lowdown: Unlike solid cuts of beef, there is no "rare" or "medium" when it comes to chicken. Chicken needs to be cooked until there is absolutely no pink left in the thickest part of the chicken piece and the juices run clear.

Bare-Bones Oven-Baked Barbecue Chicken

This here's the one to get you started, and if you do it right, bare bones is exactly what you'll be left with!

Big Daddy Lowdown: Be sure to check on the chicken every 5 minutes during the last 15 minutes of baking to keep it from burning.

1-pound chicken, quartered

SAUCE:

1/2 cup ketchup

1 dash Tabasco sauce

2 tablespoons packed light brown sugar

2 tablespoons finely minced fresh garlic

2 tablespoons Worcestershire sauce

1/4 teaspoon dry mustard

1 tablespoon vinegar

1/2 teaspoon salt

1. Preheat oven to 350°F.
2. In a saucepan, combine all the sauce ingredients. Cook over low heat for 5 minutes, stirring occasionally; set aside.
3. Place chicken pieces in large broiler pan and bake for 30 minutes without sauce. Then pour sauce over chicken and bake 30 minutes more, basting often.
    Serves 4

Beer-be-cued Chicken

1 can beer, any brand
1 tablespoon dark molasses
1 tablespoon onion juice
2 tablespoons freshly squeezed
lemon juice

1/2 cup ketchup
1 teaspoon salt
1 chicken, about 1 pound, halved

1. In a small bowl, combine the beer, molasses, onion juice, lemon juice, ketchup, and salt. Pour sauce over chicken in a shallow dish and marinate in the refrigerator 8 hours or overnight.
2. Cook on an outdoor grill approximately 1 hour or until done, turning and basting with sauce every 10 to 15 minutes.

Serves 4

Glazed Turkey Steaks

These turkey steaks can be cooked on a barbecue grill or broiled. Both methods yield equally flavorful results.

2 tablespoons orange marmalade
1 tablespoon freshly squeezed lemon
or lime juice
2 teaspoons soy sauce

1 garlic clove, minced
1/4 teaspoon curry powder
4 turkey breast tenderloins (about 4
ounces each)

1. In a small bowl, stir together marmalade, lemon or lime juice, soy sauce, garlic, and curry powder to make the glaze. Brush some of the glaze over both sides of the turkey steaks.
2. Grill turkey on an uncovered grill directly over medium flame or coals for 6 minutes. Turn and brush with glaze.

Grill 6 to 9 minutes more or until turkey is tender and no longer pink.

TO BROIL:
Place glazed turkey on the unheated rack of a broiler pan. Broil 4 to 5 inches from the heat for 3 minutes. Turn and brush with glaze. Broil 3 to 5 minutes more or until no longer pink.
Serves 4

Green Mountain Maple Barbecued Chicken

3 tablespoons pure maple syrup
3 tablespoons bottled chili sauce
1 tablespoon cider vinegar
2 teaspoons Dijon mustard

4 boneless chicken thighs
Salt and pepper to taste
1 tablespoon oil, canola or olive

1. Prepare barbecue grill to medium-high heat. In a small saucepan, stir maple syrup, chili sauce, vinegar, and mustard until well blended. Heat gently.
2. Brush chicken with oil; season with salt and pepper. Brush chicken generously with sauce; arrange chicken on barbecue. Grill about 10 minutes until cooked through, turning occasionally and brushing with more sauce. Serve immediately.
Serves 2

Herb-Tomato Grilled Chicken

3-pound chicken, cut up
Dash salt
Dash black pepper
2 tablespoons salad oil or melted
  butter

3/4 cup ketchup
2 tablespoons freshly squeezed
  lemon juice
2 garlic cloves, minced
2 teaspoons dried basil

1. Prepare barbecue grill to medium heat.
2. Cut off excess fat from chicken pieces. Loosen skin away from the meat (this helps the basting sauce reach the meat underneath). Sprinkle chicken with salt and pepper.
3. In a small bowl, combine the oil, ketchup, lemon juice, garlic, and basil; blend well to make the basting sauce.
4. Place chicken pieces on a grill rack. Brush both sides with basting sauce. Grill chicken for 12 to 15 minutes on one side, brushing with basting sauce occasionally. Turn chicken over, brush again with sauce. Grill chicken 12 to 15 minutes more or until done. Serve immediately with crusty bread and a tossed green salad, tomatoes, and crispy baked potato wedges.

Serves 8

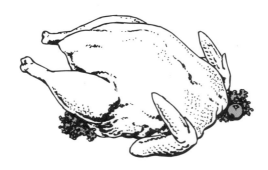

Caribbean Jerk

1 cup (2 sticks) plus 3 tablespoons butter or margarine

1/3 cup plus 3 tablespoons freshly squeezed lemon or lime juice

1 tablespoon Italian herbs, crushed

2 1/2 teaspoons salt

2 garlic cloves, crushed

3/4 teaspoon dry mustard

1/4 teaspoon coarsely ground black pepper

3 broiler-fryers (about 2 pounds each), cut in half

Salt and ground black pepper to taste

1 1/2 cups orange marmalade

1. In a small saucepan, melt butter over low heat. Stir in 1/3 cup lemon or lime juice, the Italian seasoning, salt, garlic, dry mustard, and coarse pepper to make herb butter.

2. Sprinkle each side of chicken halves lightly with salt and pepper. Place chicken, skin side up, on grill, and brush with herb butter. Grill 4 to 5 inches from medium coals or flame about 1 hour until chicken is tender, basting frequently and turning chicken occasionally.

3. Meanwhile, combine marmalade with the remaining 3 tablespoons butter and 3 tablespoons lemon or lime juice. Heat gently, stirring constantly, until melted.

4. About 4 minutes before chicken is done, brush some of the marmalade mixture on each chicken half to glaze, then grill about 1 more minute. Turn chicken, brush with remaining marmalade mixture, and grill another minute.

Serves 6

Barbecued Chicken With Sesame-Chili Sauce

Plum, sweet-and-sour, and Hoisin sauces and five-spice powder can be found in the international section of supermarkets, as well as in Asian grocery stores. The sesame-chili sauce can be made up to 5 days ahead and stored, covered, in the refrigerator. If grilling away from home, make the sauce ahead and place in a storage container. Put rinsed and dried chicken pieces into a zip-seal plastic bag. Pack the chicken and sauce on ice in a cooler.

1 jar (8 1/2 ounces) plum sauce, or
   3/4 cup sweet-and-sour sauce
1/3 cup hoisin sauce
1/3 cup soy sauce
3 tablespoons honey
4 tablespoons water
1 tablespoon sesame seed
2 garlic cloves, minced

2 teaspoons grated fresh ginger, or
   1/2 teaspoon ground ginger
1 1/2 teaspoons Oriental chili sauce,
   or several dashes Tabasco sauce
1/2 teaspoon five-spice powder
2 1/2- to 3-pound broiler-fryer,
   quartered or cut up

1. For sesame-chili sauce, in a small saucepan, combine all the ingredients except chicken. Cook over medium heat until bubbly, stirring frequently. Reduce heat. Cover and simmer for 5 minutes; set aside.
2. Rinse chicken; pat dry with paper towels. If desired, remove skin from chicken and discard. If using quartered chickens, break wing, hip, and drumstick joints so the bird will lie flat during cooking. Twist wing tips under backs.
3. Place chicken, skin side down, on an uncovered grill directly over medium coals or gas flame. Grill for 20 minutes, turn, and grill 15 to 25 minutes more, or until

chicken is tender and no longer pink inside. Brush with sauce frequently during the last 10 minutes of grilling.

4. Transfer chicken to a serving platter. Heat any remaining sauce either on the grill or stove top, and serve with chicken.

Serves 12

Chili-Basted Barbecue Chicken

The marinade may contain harmful bacteria from the raw chicken, so give the liquid enough time to get hot before removing the chicken from the grill. Discard leftover marinade.

1 cup oil, canola or olive
6 garlic cloves, pressed
1 tablespoon plus 1 teaspoon chili powder
1 tablespoon freshly squeezed lime juice
2 teaspoons ground cumin

1 teaspoon ground coriander, or a few sprigs fresh cilantro
1/2 teaspoon ground cloves
1/4 teaspoon cayenne pepper
5 pounds chicken pieces
Salt and freshly ground black pepper to taste

1. In a medium bowl, combine the first 8 ingredients (oil through cayenne pepper). Arrange chicken in a large pan in a single layer. Pour oil mixture over it. Turn chicken to coat. Cover and marinate in the refrigerator for at least 4 hours or overnight, turning occasionally.

2. Prepare barbecue grill (medium heat). Remove chicken, reserving the marinade. Season chicken with salt and pepper. Grease a grill rack and arrange chicken on rack, skin side down. Cover and grill for about 30 minutes until cooked through, basting every 10 minutes with reserved marinade, turning occasionally. Transfer to platter and serve.

Serves 8

Charcoal-Broiled Duck Breasts

4 medium duck breast fillets
4 slices bacon
Salt and pepper to taste
2 beef bouillon cubes
1 cup water
1 tablespoon red currant jelly

1/2 teaspoon dry mustard
1 tablespoon sherry
1 tablespoon brandy
1/8 teaspoon dried marjoram
1/8 teaspoon dried oregano
Grated rind of 1 orange

1. Rinse the duck and pat dry with paper towel. Wrap each fillet with a slice of bacon (as with filet mignon) and season with salt and pepper.
2. Grill over hot coals for exactly 2 minutes per side.
3. In a chafing dish or electric skillet, dissolve the bouillon cubes in water. Stir in the jelly, mustard, sherry, brandy, and spices and simmer until thickened.
4. Stir in the orange rind and add the fillets. Cook for 5 minutes or until medium rare, basting constantly.
Serves 4

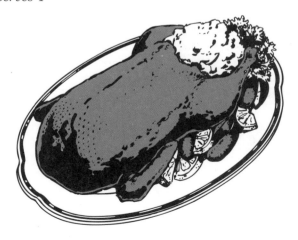

Grilled Turkey Shish Kebab

You can substitute chicken for turkey, if you wish, and use different veggies, such as red and yellow bell peppers or yellow squash.

1 1/4 pounds turkey breast tenderloins
1/3 cup bottled chili sauce
2 tablespoons freshly squeezed lemon juice
1 tablespoon sugar
2 bay leaves
8 mushrooms

8 cherry tomatoes
1 medium zucchini, cut in 1/2-inch slices
1/2 green pepper, cut in 2-inch squares
2 onions, quartered
4 skewers
2 tablespoons oil, canola or olive

1. Cut turkey tenderloins into 1 1/2-inch cubes. In a small bowl, mix the next four ingredients (chili sauce through bay leaves) to make marinade. Pour marinade over turkey cubes in a large bowl and toss to coat. Cover and marinate in the refrigerator for at least 4 hours or overnight, stirring occasionally.
2. Thread turkey and vegetables alternately on skewers. Brush lightly with oil. Broil or grill 6 inches from heat or coals for 10 minutes, turning and brushing occasionally with marinade.

Serves 4

Tasty Taco Chicken Grill

1 broiler-fryer, cut up
1 small onion, minced
1 can (8 ounces) tomato sauce
1 jar (4 ounces) taco sauce
1/4 cup molasses
2 tablespoons vinegar

1 tablespoon oil, canola or olive
1 teaspoon salt
1/2 teaspoon dried oregano
1/8 teaspoon black pepper
1/2 cup Jack cheese, grated
  (optional)

1. Preheat oven to 350°F.
2. Arrange the chicken parts in a baking dish and bake for 40 minutes. Remove from oven and cool at room temperature for 10 minutes.
3. In a small saucepan, mix together the onion, tomato sauce, taco sauce, molasses, vinegar, oil, salt, oregano, and pepper. Bring mixture to a gentle boil. Remove from heat and cool 2 minutes.
4. Pour the sauce over chicken; cover and marinate in refrigerator for at least 1 hour (overnight would be better).
5. Remove chicken from dish, draining and reserving excess sauce. Place chicken on medium-hot grill, skin side up, about 8 inches from heat. Grill, turning and brushing generously with sauce a few times, for about 20 minutes or until a fork can be inserted with ease and juices run clear. When chicken is done, place on platter and sprinkle with cheese, if desired.

Serves 8

Mesquite-Grilled Breast of Chicken with Citrus

Before chopping the lemons, limes, and oranges, use a serrated knife to cut away the rind, pits, and white membrane. Chop the remaining fruit, reserving any juice.

1 cup oil, canola or olive
2 garlic cloves, crushed
2 tablespoons minced fresh coriander
1 tablespoon thyme leaves
2 scallions, chopped
4 boneless, skinless chicken breasts (about 1/2 pound each), halved
2 shallots, minced
1 teaspoon minced fresh ginger
2 tablespoons unsalted butter
2 lemons, peeled and chopped

2 limes, peeled and chopped
2 oranges, peeled and chopped
2 cups chicken broth
1 teaspoon cornstarch
1 teaspoon water
1/4 cup plus 2 tablespoons Grand Marnier
White pepper to taste
Salt to taste
1 lemon, cut into wedges

1. In a ceramic or glass bowl, combine the oil, garlic, coriander, thyme, and scallions. Add chicken breasts, turning to coat. Cover and marinate in the refrigerator for at least 8 hours or overnight.

2. In a saucepan, cook the shallots and ginger in the butter over low heat, stirring, until the shallots are softened. Add the chopped lemons, limes, and oranges with all the reserved juices, and simmer the mixture for 10 to 12 minutes or until the liquid is reduced to a syrupy consistency.

3. Add the broth, increase the heat to moderate, and boil the mixture, stirring occasionally, for 10 to 15 minutes or until it is reduced by one-third. Mix the cornstarch and water together. Stir in the cornstarch mixture and

simmer for 30 seconds. Strain through a fine sieve into a bowl. Add the Grand Marnier, white pepper, and salt to taste; set aside.

4. Remove chicken from the marinade and let it stand at room temperature for 15 minutes. Grill the chicken on a rack set about 5 inches above mesquite coals, for 10 to 12 minutes or until it is just cooked through, turning once. Transfer the chicken to a platter, spoon the sauce over it, and garnish the platter with lemon wedges.
    Serves 4

River City Rubs—Simon Guzman and Theron Malone

River City Rub's Smoked Chicken

1 large chicken, cut up into pieces
   (3 to 5 pounds)
1 cup of River City Chicken Rub (see
   page 20)

Barbecue sauce, homemade or
   bottled (optional)

MARINADE:
1 cup Italian dressing
1/2 cup Worcestershire sauce

1/2 cup soy sauce

1. In a small bowl, mix the marinade ingredients. Place
    chicken in a zip-seal bag and pour marinade over
    chicken. Marinate in the refrigerator for at least
    4 hours.
2. Prepare smoker to cook at 225°F. Remove chicken
    from marinade and lightly sprinkle rub over both
    sides of chicken. Place chicken in smoker and add
    4 chunks of apple wood and continue to cook for 3 1/2
    hours or until chicken reaches an internal
    temperature of 180°F.
3. If desired, add barbecue sauce to chicken the last 10 to
    20 minutes of cooking time.
    Serves 4 to 6

6
Pork—Out of the Barrel

If you're looking for a quick and easy meal, chops, tenderloin, ground pork, and ham steaks can be barbecued in 15 to 30 minutes. Experiment with the different rubs and sauces from Chapter 1. Marinating beforehand or brushing with sauce while on the grill will enhance the flavor of your dish. But be careful not to overdo it with fast-cooking pork cuts. Monitor the pork with a meat thermometer and remove the meat from the grill the moment its internal temperature reaches 160°F, unless the recipe says otherwise. By following that simple rule, you're sure to enjoy a tender, juicy meal every time. If you're up to the challenge of something a little more complicated, some of these can get pretty involved (especially the Chinese dishes)—but they're worth it.

Barbecued Pork Roast

For indirect roasting, put an aluminum pan directly under
the roast and arrange coals on either side of the pan.

3 pounds center-cut pork loin	8 peppercorns
1 tablespoon dried sage	1 tablespoon seasoned salt
1 teaspoon ground allspice	1 cup applesauce
1 teaspoon ground coriander	1/2 cup packed brown sugar
1 teaspoon ground nutmeg	

1. Rinse and pat dry pork roast; set aside. In a food
   processor, combine sage, allspice, coriander, nutmeg,
   peppercorns, and seasoned salt. Pulse until spices are
   combined.
2. Press spices on fat cap of roast. Place in domed
   barbecue grill and cook by indirect roasting for about
   1 1/2 hours.
3. Combine applesauce and brown sugar. Coat the top of
   the roast during the last 30 minutes of cooking,
   applying the applesauce mixture until it is used up.
   Continue roasting until the meat reaches an internal
   temperature of 170°F.
4. Remove roast from grill and let stand for 15 minutes
   before carving.
   Serves 6

Oriental Barbecue Pork Tenderloin

If you can't find toasted sesame oil with the other oils in the supermarket, look in the Oriental foods aisle or visit an Asian grocery store.

8-pound boneless pork tenderloin
2/3 cup soy sauce
2/3 cup Oriental toasted sesame oil
4 large garlic cloves, minced

1 teaspoon grated fresh ginger
1 teaspoon MSG (optional)
1 bottle (19-ounces) barbecue
  sauce, any brand

1. Trim pork tenderloin of all fat (the sesame oil will prevent burning on the grill).
2. In a deep bowl, combine 1/3 cup of the soy sauce, 1/3 cup of sesame oil, 3 minced garlic cloves, ginger, and MSG (if used). Mix well, making sure the ginger does not clump. Add pork to marinade, cover, and marinate in the refrigerator for at least 6 hours or overnight.
3. Remove pork from marinade and place it on a barbecue grill. Discard marinade. Add wet wood to grill pan to ensure adequate supply of smoke. Cover and cook for 1 1/2 hours or until meat has reached an internal temperature of 170°F.
4. Combine barbecue sauce, 1/3 cup sesame oil, 1/3 cup soy sauce, and 1 minced garlic clove in a bowl, mixing well. Serve over sliced pork tenderloins.
   Serves 8

Chinese Barbecued Pork (Cha Siu)

This dish can be served as a main course or used as an ingredient in other recipes, some of which appear in this chapter. Since barbecued pork freezes well in an airtight container for up to three months (or refrigerated for a week), you can simply heat some up and impress your mother-in-law when she pays one of her surprise visits (unless, of course, you want to discourage said visits).

1 pound lean pork butt
1/4 teaspoon salt
Dash pepper
1 1/4 tablespoons sugar
2 teaspoons low-sodium soy sauce
1 teaspoon roasting salt

1 1/2 teaspoons oyster sauce
1 1/2 teaspoons hoisin sauce
2 teaspoons white wine
1 tablespoon honey
1 cup water (for roasting)

1. Cut meat into pieces, approximately 5 x 2 x 1 inches.
2. Sprinkle meat with next 9 ingredients (salt through honey), mixing well. Cover and marinate in the refrigerator for at least 5 hours or overnight.
3. Preheat oven to 375°F.
4. Add water to roasting pan and insert rack. Place pork on rack and roast uncovered for 30 minutes per side, basting with liquid in pan three or four times.
   Serves 5

Chinese Barbecued Pork Bun (Cha Siu Bow)

If you're going to prepare this or any Asian recipe and you don't own a wok, go buy one. You can get an electric version or one that sits on the stove directly or atop a special metallic ring that comes with it. While you're in the cookware department, buy a steamer—a pot, a metal colander that fits inside, and a tight-fitting lid with an adjustable vent.

1/3 cup warm water
1/2 teaspoon sugar
1 package dry yeast
2 1/2 cups all-purpose flour
2 1/2 cups cake flour
4 tablespoons sugar

1/2 teaspoon salt
2 tablespoons shortening
1 1/4 cups low-fat milk (1% or 2%)
16 pieces parchment paper, 2 inches square

FILLING:
1 tablespoon salad oil
6 ounces Chinese barbecued pork (Cha Siu), diced (see previous recipe)
2 teaspoons water
1/2 teaspoon salt

1/2 teaspoon sugar
1/2 teaspoon low-sodium soy sauce
1 teaspoon oyster sauce
1 teaspoon hoisin sauce
2 teaspoons cornstarch
4 teaspoons cold water

1. In an 8-ounce measuring cup, mix the water, sugar, and yeast. Let stand until mixture rises to the 8-ounce level, about 20 minutes.
2. Sift the flour, cake flour, sugar, and salt into a large mixing bowl. Add the shortening, yeast mixture, and milk. Knead 5 minutes to form dough. Cover with a damp cloth and set dough in a warm place. Allow the

dough to rise for 3 hours.

3. To make the filling, heat a wok, add the oil, and stir-fry pork for 2 minutes. Add water, salt, sugar, soy sauce, oyster sauce, and hoisin sauce. Bring to a boil.

4. In a cup, mix the cornstarch and 4 teaspoons of cold water. Add to wok, stir, and cook for 1 minute. Cool in refrigerator before using.

5. Once the dough is raised, shape it into rolls about 2 inches in diameter. Cut each roll into 1 1/2-inch pieces; shape each piece into a shallow bowl shape.

6. Place 1 tablespoon of filling in the center of each bowl, then close and twist dough to form a bun. Put the bun on a square of parchment paper (this prevents the bun from becoming soggy while steaming). Place 8 buns in a pie pan and allow them to set and rise for 15 minutes in a warm place.

7. Steam for 25 minutes.

Makes 16 buns

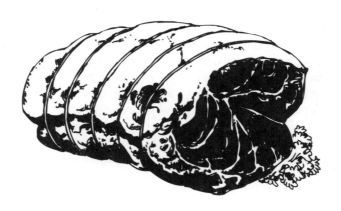

Pueblo Barbecued Pork Roast

Small, aromatic juniper berries originally were used to flavor gin but also are used in pickling mixtures and to season poultry, pork, and game. Dried juniper berries are sold in the spice section of the grocery store.

1/4 cup oil, canola or olive
1 1/2 cups chopped yellow onion
3 garlic cloves, minced
4 dried juniper berries, crushed
1/2 teaspoon coriander seed, crushed
1 bay leaf
4 large, ripe tomatoes, quartered and seeded
1 1/4 cups water

2/3 cup cider vinegar
1/3 to 1/2 cup honey
1 tablespoon ground red chili powder
1 tablespoon red chili flakes
2 teaspoons salt
1 ounce unsweetened chocolate (1 square), grated
4- to 5-pound pork rib roast

1. In a large, heavy saucepan over medium heat, heat the oil and sauté the onions until soft. Add garlic, juniper berries, coriander seed, and bay leaf; sauté 2 to 3 minutes longer. Add tomatoes, water, vinegar, honey, powdered chili and flakes, and salt. Simmer, covered, 30 minutes. Add chocolate and simmer, uncovered, 20 to 30 minutes more, until sauce is fairly thick.
2. Preheat oven to 350°F.
3. Place roast, fat side up, in a roasting pan and baste generously with the sauce. Roast for about 3 hours, basting occasionally with sauce and pan drippings. Let roast stand for 10 minutes in a warm place before carving. Slice roast and spoon additional sauce over each portion.
   Serves 6

Rotisserie Barbecued Leg of Pork

9- to 11-pound leg of pork
1 cup packed brown sugar
2 teaspoons all-purpose flour

1 teaspoon dry mustard
1/4 cup vinegar
1/4 teaspoon ground cloves

1. Insert rotisserie rod through center of meat and place on rotisserie grill whose coals have burned down to red, glowing ash. If using a meat thermometer, angle it so the tip rests in the center of meat but not in fat or on the rod, and roast to 170°F. If you have no thermometer, roast 3 1/2 to 4 hours, depending on size of meat.
2. In a small bowl, combine the sugar, flour, dry mustard, vinegar, and cloves and brush on roast frequently during the last 30 minutes of cooking.
    Serves about 20

River City Rub's Boston Butt

6- to 7-pound Boston Butt
1 cup of River City Pork Rub (see page 20)

1/4 cup of prepared yellow mustard
Barbecue sauce

1. Prepare pork butt with a light coating of mustard. Place an even, heavy coating of rub over the meat.
2. Prepare smoker with charcoal and wood. When the smoker reaches 225°F, place pork butt inside and cook until the internal temperature reaches 160°F, about 4 to 5 hours or when the butt is very dark in color.
3. Wrap the butt in foil. Place the butt back into the smoker and continue cooking until the internal temperature reaches 195°F, about 4 to 5 more hours.

> **Big Daddy Lowdown:** Cook meat around 1 1/2 hours per pound. (For a 7-pound butt, cook for about 10 hours.)

4. Let cool slightly and trim any fat. Pull the pork and serve hot on a bun with your favorite barbecue sauce. *Serves 10 to 12*

Butts in a Bag!

Remus Powers, Ph.B., known in some circles as Ardie A. Davis, did a heck of a job writing the foreword for the book you're now holding in your hands. The man knows more about barbecue than most folks have forgotten, and being that he's a Doctor of Barbecue Philosophy, I think it's best to let him speak for himself:

Southerners have used this method for years, although I haven't seen much use of it in the sport barbecue network since heavy-duty aluminum foil took over in popularity.

It is simple, and has never failed me over the past twenty years. I learned about it from a cook at the Memphis in May World Championship Barbecue. We were sipping cold beer and visiting. When it came time to check the butts in his cooker, I went along. Those beautiful butts had been cooking for I don't know how long, but they weren't ready yet. No problem. He took them off the rack and put each one in a small brown-paper bag like you get at the supermarket. Each butt cooked in its own bag. When he took those butts out a few hours later I happened to be there. They were bone-slippin' tender, moist, and oh, so flavorful.

Now it's time to let the butt out of the bag, so to speak. Mind you, every cook has their own way of doing it, but here's mine:

Remus's Easy Recipe for Barbecue Butts in a Bag

I use a plain old Weber kettle cooker. You can adapt this recipe to your own cooker.

INGREDIENTS

Charcoal—your favorite brand that works for you. I use Kingsford most often, or Royal Oak when I can get it, or sometimes the cheap supermarket brand.

Four cups of water-soaked wood chips, half apple and half pecan, or your own favorite smoke. Soak overnight or a minimum of 30 minutes. Drain first water off after 30 minutes, then add more fresh water; makes for a more mellow smoke.

One, two, or more big pork butts, aka pork shoulders, as big as you like.

Pork rub—your favorite brand, such as Bad Byron's Butt Rub, or Jim Tabb's Pig Powder, or your own homemade rub. This is optional.

A brown-paper grocery bag for each butt; some cooks use double bags.

1. Ignite charcoal in a chimney starter and let it burn until covered with gray ash, then dump and bank it on one end of your kettle to avoid grease fires during the cooking process. Put the drained wood chips directly atop the hot charcoal. Quickly put the grill grate on and place butts on the end opposite the fire.
2. Lid the cooker. If your hood is like mine and doesn't have a built-in thermometer, stick a candy thermo-

meter in the lid vent hole to monitor temperatures. Allow the temperature to crank up to at least 350°F for the first 30 to 45 minutes, then help it descend to 250°F by adjusting the vent holes in the bottom of the cooker. This puts a bark on your butt early on.

3. After 4 hours or so, put one butt in each bag and return them to their same place in the cooker, opposite the fire.

4. Depending upon the weight and quality of your butts, you'll have tender, delicious barbecue ready for pickin' in another 4 to 5 or more hours. When it's easy to pull, it's done. If you can pull the shoulder blade out smoothly without coaxing, you know you have mastered the art of cooking butt!

Most sport cooks rub their butts with secret seasonings several hours before cooking. They may also spray or mop their butts with apple juice or seasoned apple cider vinegar or another vinegar or mustard base mopping sauce occasionally during the cooking process. That's optional as far as I'm concerned, especially after the butts are bagged. Try one butt with seasoning and one without, and decide which one you like best.

People ask me, "Won't the bags catch on fire?" All I can say is it hasn't happened yet!

Yield will vary depending on meat size and quantity.

Smitty's Award-Winning Bar-B-Que Pork Tenderloin

Brian Smith and his team, Smitty's Bar-B-Que, know how to have a good time, they know how to tell a good story, and after spending a good part of the weekend with them in Lenexa sampling each of their Barbecue Battle entries, to say that they know how to handle themselves in competition is only gonna get us halfway there. These boys absolutely spoiled us with some delicious samples, and their award-winning pork tenderloin was so good that we had them throw on a second one, and videotaped them, just to make sure we could try to come close to it when we tried it on our own.

2 2-pound pork tenderloins	4 tablespoons packed brown sugar
1 pound of thick cut bacon	2 tablespoons sugar
1/3 cup Dijon mustard	2 tablespoons kosher salt
Apple-mango juice, in spray bottle	1 teaspoon ground cumin
2 cups barbecue sauce (optional)	1 teaspoon black pepper
4 tablespoons paprika	1 teaspoon cayenne pepper

1. In a small bowl, mix last 7 ingredients (paprika through cayenne pepper). Coat mixture evenly over pork tenderloins, place in a zip-seal bag, and let marinate in the refrigerator overnight.
2. Empty one bag of hickory chunks into a bucket filled with water. Let soak overnight.
3. Remove tenderloin from bag, coat with Dijon mustard. Wrap each piece in bacon from end to end.
4. Ignite charcoal in a chimney starter. Brian suggests letting it burn for the amount of time it takes the average guy to drink a 12-ounce cold beverage, before

placing several chunks of the wet hickory onto the coals. Maintain a temperature of about 220°F.

5. Place meat on rack, allow to cook at 2 hours per pound, about 4 hours total.

6. After about 3 hours, spray meat with apple-mango juice.

7. Remove meat and unwrap bacon. If using barbecue sauce, heat in a small saucepan before serving. Slice the meat and enjoy. The bacon can be eaten on the spot or crumbled up and used to make a batch of smoky baked beans.

Serves 6 to 10

7

Fishin' for Good Barbecue

As every chef and fisherman knows, seafood tastes best when eaten within a day or two of being caught. But taste isn't the only reason to seek out the freshest seafood you can find. Seafood is particularly vulnerable to contamination and spoilage. Fresh seafood is practically odorless, so if the place you're buying it from reeks with a fishy smell, take your business elsewhere. Cooked shrimp, steamed clams, and other cooked items should not be situated below or be in direct contact with raw seafood in the display case. The person weighing your order should be wearing a clean pair of plastic gloves.

In this chapter, you'll find several shrimp recipes. Shrimp can be purchased whole or already peeled and deveined. Devein means to remove the intestine—the dark line running down the critter's back. To remove it yourself, you'll need a sharp paring knife or a deveining tool, which has a skinny, curved blade. If using a paring knife, peel the shrimp and make a shallow cut down its back to expose the intestine. Then, using the knife, a toothpick, or your fingers, gently pull the intestine out. If using a deveining tool, you don't need to remove the shell beforehand. Insert the blade under the shell and make your shallow cut from head to tail. As you do this, the intestine will stick to the serrated part of the knife as the sharp, upper edge splits the shell open.

Barbecued Tuna Burgers

This recipe can also be made with canned salmon.

Big Daddy Lowdown: Tuna burgers might stick to the barbecue grill and fall apart when you attempt to turn them. To prevent this mess, cover the grill with nonstick aluminum foil (or regular foil coated with cooking spray) before heating. Or broil them in the oven, turning once.

---

1 can (6 1/2 ounces) tuna, chunk
  light in water, drained
1 cup bread crumbs, plain or savory
1 egg, slightly beaten
1/2 cup minced celery
1/2 cup mayonnaise, regular or
  flavored

1/4 cup minced onion
Crisp leaf lettuce (like romaine or
  iceberg)
4 hamburger buns, toasted
1 tomato, sliced (optional)

1. In a medium-size bowl, mash tuna with a fork. Mix in bread crumbs, egg, celery, mayonnaise, and onion. Form into 4 patties.
2. Barbecue or fry 3 to 4 minutes on each side until cooked through. Serve patties on lettuce-lined buns, and garnish with sliced tomatoes and additional mayonnaise, if desired.
   Serves 4

Basic Barbecued Salmon Steaks

When barbecuing fish steaks, make sure the grill is well oiled. Or cover the grill with a well-oiled layer of heavy-duty aluminum foil or use a grill-safe pan.

4 salmon steaks
1/4 cup oil, olive or canola
2 tablespoons freshly squeezed
  lemon juice

2 tablespoons soy sauce
1/2 tablespoon ground ginger

1. Place the salmon steaks in a shallow dish. In a small bowl, combine oil, lemon juice, soy sauce, and ginger and pour over the steaks. Cover and marinate in the refrigerator for 30 minutes; turn steaks and marinate 30 minutes more.
2. Barbecue 10 minutes on well-oiled grill; turn steaks, brush with marinade, and cook 10 minutes more.
   Serves 4

Ginger-Lime Swordfish Steaks

Swordfish, like other fish steaks, should be cooked over moderately high heat. In general, fish needs about 10 minutes of cooking per inch of thickness (when measured at the thickest point). Turn the fish steak once during cooking if it is more than an inch thick; thinner pieces don't need to be turned at all. To keep flavor and moisture in, do not pierce the fish while it is cooking. You'll know it's done when the fish turns opaque and starts to flake when tested with a fork. To prevent sticking, oil the grill, rack, or basket just before placing seafood on the barbecue.

1 1/2 pounds swordfish steaks,
  1 inch thick
1/4 cup freshly squeezed lime juice
2 tablespoons olive oil
1 teaspoon finely chopped fresh
  ginger

1/4 teaspoon salt
Dash cayenne pepper
1 garlic clove, crushed
1 lime, cut into wedges

1. Cut each fish steak into 3 to 4 pieces. In shallow glass dish, combine the remaining ingredients except for lime wedges. Place fish in dish; turn to coat with marinade. Cover and marinate in the refrigerator for at least 1 hour.

2. Remove fish from marinade. Cook on oiled grill about 4 inches from medium-hot coals or flame for about 10 minutes, brushing 2 to 3 times with reserved marinade. If not cooked through after 10 minutes, turn once and brush with marinade. Fish is done when it flakes with fork. Serve with lime wedges.

Serves 6

Big Daddy's Char-Broiled Shrimp

You can buy precooked shrimp, but raw shrimp that you buy and cook yourself tastes better. If you've never deveined raw shrimp before, the introduction to this chapter tells you how.

Big Daddy Lowdown: When buying shrimp, ask for a bag of ice to keep your order cold; if the weather is particularly hot, put a cooler with ice in the back of your pickup to carry the shrimp home in. Refrigerate the shrimp until you are ready to prepare it.

1 cup olive oil
1/3 cup chopped fresh parsley
2 tablespoons freshly squeezed
   lemon juice
2 garlic cloves, crushed

1 teaspoon salt
3 pounds large, fresh shrimp, peeled
   and deveined, tails intact
8 bamboo skewers, soaked in water
   30 minutes

1. In a 13 x 9 x 2-inch baking dish, combine the oil, parsley, lemon juice, garlic, and salt, stirring well. Add shrimp, stirring gently; cover and marinate in the refrigerator for at least 8 hours, stirring occasionally.
2. Using a slotted spoon, remove shrimp from dish; reserve marinade. Thread shrimp on skewers and grill over medium-hot coals or flame 3 to 4 minutes per side, basting frequently with marinade. Be careful not to overcook.

Serves 8

Grilled Curry-Apricot Shrimp and Scallop Kebabs

Bamboo skewers should be completely submerged in water for 30 minutes before use to prevent them from burning on the grill.

1/2 cup olive oil	4 teaspoons fresh minced and
1/2 cup apricot preserves	seeded jalapeño pepper
2 tablespoons Dijon mustard	16 large shrimp, peeled and
2 tablespoons curry powder	deveined, tails intact
2 tablespoons minced garlic	12 sea scallops
2 tablespoons chopped fresh cilantro	4 bamboo skewers, soaked in water
	30 minutes

1. In a medium bowl, combine the first 7 ingredients (oil through jalapeño). Add the shrimp and scallops, tossing to coat. Cover and marinate in the refrigerator 30 minutes to 1 hour, tossing occasionally.
2. Prepare barbecue. Thread 4 shrimp and 3 scallops alternately on each skewer. Grill for about 3 minutes per side until shrimp are just cooked through and scallops are opaque, brushing frequently with marinade.
3. Bring the remaining marinade to simmer in a small saucepan. Serve kebabs, with marinade on side.
Serves 4

Lemon-Herb Barbecued Shrimp

1 1/2 cups ketchup
1/2 cup white vinegar
1/4 large lemon, seeded and finely minced, including rind
1 tablespoon Gravy Master or Kitchen Bouquet browning and seasoning sauce
1 teaspoon sugar
1 teaspoon ground coriander

1/2 teaspoon ground cumin
1/4 teaspoon ground ginger
1/8 teaspoon paprika
Cayenne pepper to taste
20 to 25 large shrimp (2 pounds), shelled and deveined
6 to 8 bamboo skewers, soaked in water 30 minutes

1. In a small saucepan, make marinade by mixing the first 10 ingredients (ketchup through cayenne pepper). Simmer 15 minutes, stirring frequently.
2. Thread shrimp onto skewers and brush with marinade; place on grill 4 to 6 inches from hot glowing coals. Cook for 3 to 5 minutes until shrimp are done, turning and brushing frequently with marinade. Be careful not to overcook.

Serves 6 to 8

Hot 'n Spicy Barbecued Shrimp

1/2 cup oil, canola or olive
1/2 cup chili sauce or salsa
1/2 cup ketchup
1/3 cup freshly squeezed lemon juice
1/4 cup Worcestershire sauce
2 tablespoons GravyMaster or
   Kitchen Bouquet browning and
   seasoning sauce
1 teaspoon soy sauce

1 teaspoon Tabasco sauce
2 tablespoons minced garlic
1 tablespoon packed dark brown
   sugar
1 lemon, cut in wedges
20 to 25 large shrimp (2 pounds),
   shelled and deveined
8 bamboo skewers, soaked in water
   30 minutes

1. In a bowl, combine the first 10 ingredients (oil through
    brown sugar) and mix well. Place shrimp in a zip-seal
    bag, add marinade, close bag, and marinate in the
    refrigerator for 24 hours, turning several times.
2. Remove shrimp from marinade and drain; thread on
    skewers with lemon wedges. Broil or grill 4 to 5 inches
    from heat source for 3 to 5 minutes until shrimp are
    done, turning and basting frequently. Be careful not to
    overcook.

Serves 6 to 8

Louisiana-Style Barbecued Catfish in Tomato Sauce

1 cup finely chopped onion
1 cup fresh parsley sprigs
2 tablespoons oil, olive or peanut
1 tablespoon finely chopped garlic
4 cups peeled and cubed fresh
   tomatoes

Salt and ground red pepper to taste
2 cups burgundy wine
1 tablespoon soy sauce
4 catfish fillets (up to 1/2 pound
   each)

1. Sauté onions and parsley in oil for 3 to 5 minutes. Add garlic, tomatoes, salt, pepper, wine, and soy sauce and cook for about 10 minutes, until the onions are translucent.
2. Lightly season fillets with salt and red pepper. On well-oiled, medium-hot grill, place fish fillets, skin side up, for 3 minutes. Turn and cook 2 minutes more.
3. Transfer fish to an aluminum foil boat or grill-safe pan and top with sauce. Place back on grill and close barbecue cover. Cook 10 minutes more.
    Serves 4

Steamed Fish and Spinach

1 package (16-ounces) frozen fish
  fillets, thawed
1/2 cup chopped yellow onion
1 garlic clove, minced
1 tablespoon oil, olive or canola
1/4 cup dry white wine
1/4 teaspoon dried tarragon or basil

1/8 teaspoon salt
1/8 teaspoon black pepper
1 package (10-ounces) frozen
  chopped spinach, thawed, well
  drained
1 bell pepper, green or red, cut into
  thin strips

1. Cut block of fish crosswise into 4 equal pieces. In a small skillet, cook onion and garlic in hot oil until tender. Remove from heat. Stir in wine, tarragon or basil, salt, and pepper. Return to heat and boil gently for about 2 minutes or until most of the liquid has evaporated. Remove skillet from heat; set aside.
2. Place 1/8 of the spinach on four 12 x 18-inch pieces of heavy foil. Place 1 portion of fish on each portion of spinach. Spoon the onion mixture evenly over fish. Top with remaining spinach and the bell pepper strips. Bring up long edges of foil, leaving a little space for steam expansion, and seal tightly with a double fold. Then fold short ends to seal. Grill foil packets, seam side up, directly over medium coals for about 10 minutes; turn and cook 10 minutes more or until fish flakes easily with a fork.

Serves 4

Whole Flounder with Herb Marinade

Almost any fresh herb works well with this recipe. Try rosemary, cilantro, dill, basil, parsley, or a combination of two or three different herbs.

3 tablespoons olive oil
2 tablespoons chopped fresh herbs
1 teaspoon minced garlic
1/4 teaspoon salt

Black pepper to taste
2-pound whole flounder, scales
    removed

1. In a small bowl, combine the oil, herbs, garlic, salt, and pepper; set aside for up to 2 hours.
2. Rinse fish well under running water and pat dry with a paper towel. Using a sharp fillet or paring knife, slash the thicker part of both fillets with 1 or 2 shallow diagonal cuts through the skin and into the meat. Set aside 1 tablespoon of marinade, and rub the rest all over the surface of the fish and into the cuts. Set on plate and refrigerate for 15 minutes.
3. Build a medium-hot fire in a charcoal grill. Oil the grill rack, and place the fish dark-skin side down. Grill 4 minutes or until skin releases easily from grill. Turn, baste with any marinade remaining on the plate, and continue grilling until a thin skewer easily penetrates thickest part of the fish, another 2 to 4 minutes.
    Serves 2

Summer Smoked Sea Bass and Black Grapes

From *Get Smokin'* by Cookshack, Inc.
© 2000 by Cookshack, Inc.
Reprinted by permission of Running Press,
a member of Perseus Books, L.L.C.

2 fresh sea bass
Black pepper to taste

1 cup freshly picked black grapes, thinly sliced
Caesar salad, lightly seasoned

HONEY DIJON DRESSING:

1 cup olive oil
1/4 cup red wine vinegar
1/4 cup honey
2 tablespoons Dijon mustard
Juice of 2 lemons

3 tablespoons poppy seeds
2 tablespoons chopped fresh parsley
Chopped pulp of 1/2 lemon
2 tablespoons freshly cracked blacked pepper

1. In a medium bowl, combine the first 5 dressing ingredients and blend well. Add poppy seeds, parsley, lemon pulp, and pepper. Mix well; set aside.
2. Butterfly sea bass. Open fish and lightly season with black pepper. Add a layer of grapes; close fish.
3. Place fish in a zip-seal bag, add half the honey dijon dressing, and marinate overnight in the refrigerator.
4. Smoke-cook with hickory wood at 200°F for 45 to 60 minutes.
5. Ladle remaining honey dijon dressing onto warm plates. Lay fish in center. Surround with Caesar salad.
6. Garnish with a small cluster of smoked grapes and fresh watercress if desired.
   Serves 2

Barbecued Oysters in the Shell

From *Seafood Grilling Twice a Week* by Evie Hansen, reprinted with permission. You should check out their website at www.seafoodeducators.com. In addition to recipes and tips, they've got an easy solution for all you grillers looking to take on smoker dishes—
Captain H's Grill Smoker.

12 large, 20 medium, or 32 small oysters in the shell

1 cup preferred barbecue sauce

1. Scrub oyster shells thoroughly with a scrub brush.
2. Crumple a sheet of heavy-duty aluminum foil, place on grill, and lay oysters lid side up in indentations of foil. (Indentations will keep oysters from tipping and spilling their liquid.)

Big Daddy Lowdown: Oysters in the shell have two sides: a lid that is flat and a cup that is bowl-shaped. To make sure the natural juices in the oysters are retained, be sure to place them on the grill as directed.

3. Grill for 5 to 15 minutes or until shells begin to open. (The larger the oyster, the longer the cooking time.)
4. Place an oyster knife under the lid of each oyster and pry off the top shell.
5. Top with your favorite barbecue sauce.
   Serves 4

Soft-Shelled Crab on a Bed of Spinach

Also from *Seafood Grilling Twice a Week*,
reprinted with permission.

4 soft-shelled crabs, cleaned	4 cups spinach leaves, washed, dried
Vegetable oil	1 cup carrots, grated
1/4 teaspoon salt	1 cup grapes, halved
1/4 teaspoon pepper	1/3 cup light poppy seed dressing

1. Lightly coat crabs with vegetable oil. Season with salt and pepper.
2. Place crabs upside down on grill for 4 minutes. Turn and grill for 4 minutes more.
3. Divide spinach, carrots, and grapes on 4 plates. Place crab on top.
4. Drizzle poppy seed dressing over top.
   Serves 4

Clambake

Some of the best seafood I have ever eaten was cooked at a clambake. Michael Greenwald, the author of *The Cruising Chef Cookbook*, was gracious enough to share his "recipe" with us. The thing about a clambake is that it's more of a ritual than it is a recipe. All you really need are lots of clams and potatoes—the rest is up to you.

INSTRUCTIONS

Traditionally, a pit about 18 inches deep is dug in the sand and lined with flat rocks or bricks. The pit requires 8 to 10 pounds of rocks per square foot. A big fire is built and allowed to burn for at least an hour, adding fuel steadily to make a good bed of coals. When the coals are ready, sweep them toward the edges of the pit to expose the hot rocks. Lay down a 6-inch layer of seaweed or chopped lettuce.

Food is added to the pit in a single layer. Brush small or medium potatoes with oil or butter, wrap in foil, pierce many times with a fork, and place on the stones, close to the coals. Corn in the husk also goes here.

Fish is usually cut into individual portions and wrapped in foil. Chopped vegetables such as summer squash and tomatoes are often enclosed with the fish.

If pork is included, it is usually cut into individual portions and wrapped loosely in foil. Traditionally the pork is roasted separately while the pit steams.

If live crabs are on the menu they should be contained in a mesh sack. Place whole fish that have been gutted and scaled directly on the clams or crabs. Traditionally the fish are wrapped in banana leaves to make handling easier. You can use foil but leaves are much better.

After you have added all your food, cover with a 4-inch layer of seaweed. The briny steam from seaweed enhances the flavor of the food. Clean wet burlap sacks are placed on top of the seaweed to close the pit and contain the steam and heat. Allow at least 3 hours for steaming—resist the temptation to take a peek!

As soon as the pit is opened and the food removed, turn the seaweed back, sweep the coals over all, and throw on more wood. You will need heat to toast those marshmallows later on! When everything is cooked, sit down and enjoy the feast. Be sure to have a big pot of melted butter, coleslaw, and lots of cold drinks on hand.

8
Something Different

If you're looking for something new for your barbecue, you've hit pay dirt with this chapter. Here you'll find some of my favorite recipes for stews, veggies, and other off-the-beaten-track dishes. But being a deer hunter myself, my top pick is barbecued venison. You may prefer farm-raised venison, which is particularly tender and delicately flavored and doesn't need marinating unless you want to vary the flavor. According to the Maine Deer and Elk Farmers Association, venison is not only high in protein, it contains iron, zinc, B vitamins, and is raised naturally, without growth hormones, antibiotics, and dyes. When grilling, venison should be cooked quickly over high heat and then removed from heat, covered with foil, and allowed to rest for 5 to 10 minutes before serving. The association also points out that venison is a dense meat; a small portion may be all you need.

Fiery Barbecued Venison

This Southwestern-style dish packs an intense flavor punch. The heat is countered somewhat by the coriander avocado cream.

2 teaspoons paprika
1 teaspoon chili powder
1 teaspoon ground cumin
1 teaspoon ground coriander
1 teaspoon sugar
1 teaspoon salt
1/2 teaspoon dry mustard

1/2 teaspoon dried thyme
1/2 teaspoon good curry powder
1/2 teaspoon cayenne pepper
4 venison steaks or medallions
   (about 4 ounces per portion)
Olive oil (for basting)

CORIANDER AVOCADO CREAM:
1/2 ripe avocado, peeled (about 4 tablespoons)
3 tablespoons dairy sour cream
2 tablespoons chopped fresh cilantro

1/2 teaspoon lime zest (grated lime peel)
4 drops Tabasco sauce
Dash salt and pepper

1. In a large bowl, combine the first 10 ingredients (paprika through cayenne pepper). Place venison in the bowl and mix to coat well. Brush off excess coating and let stand in the refrigerator for 1 hour.
2. Oil the barbecue grill and heat. Brown the venison well over high heat, turning often and basting lightly with olive oil. When done, remove from grill, cover with foil, and let stand about 5 minutes.
3. To make the avocado cream, place avocado, sour cream, cilantro, lime peel, Tabasco sauce, salt, and pepper in a food processor or electric blender and blend until smooth. Serve with barbecued venison.
    Serves 4

Slow-Cooked Venison Barbecue

Any red meat can be substituted for venison. Cut the meat into 1-inch cubes before putting it into the slow cooker.

3 pounds venison stew meat
1 cup diced yellow onion
4 garlic cloves, chopped
1 cup red wine vinegar
1/2 cup Worcestershire sauce
2 teaspoons meat seasoning (such as Lawry's Natural Choice)

2 teaspoons seasoned salt (Lawry's or other brand)
1 pound bacon, cooked and crumbled
2 cups ketchup
1/2 cup molasses
1/2 cup packed light brown sugar

1. Place venison, onion, garlic, vinegar, Worcestershire sauce, and seasoning in a slow cooker. Cook on High for 1 to 2 hours until meat is cooked and tender.
2. Add bacon, ketchup, molasses, and brown sugar. Turn slow cooker on Low and cook 4 to 6 hours more. Serve over rice, potatoes, or toast.

Serves 7

Smoked Pheasant with Cabernet Sauce

From *Get Smokin'* by Cookshack, Inc.
© 2000 by Cookshack, Inc. Reprinted by permission of
Running Press, a member of Perseus Books, L.L.C.

Always use a good grade of wine as it adds richness to the sauce.

12 pheasant breasts with wing
   sections
3 cups cabernet sauvignon
1/3 cup red wine vinegar
1 tablespoon chopped fresh sage

1 tablespoon chopped fresh thyme
1 tablespoon salt
1 tablespoon cracked black pepper
1/4 cup olive oil

CABERNET SAUCE:
3 cups demi-glace
1 cup cabernet sauvignon

1 cup sliced mushrooms

1. Wash pheasant and pat dry; place in a pan just big
    enough for pheasant.
2. In a small bowl, mix the next 7 ingredients and pour
    mixture over the pheasant, turning to coat. Let
    marinate in the refrigerator for 24 hours.
3. Remove pheasant from marinade and place on hot
    charbroiler. Cook for 10 minutes on each side.
4. Load in smoker. Smoke over apple wood at 200°F for
    2 1/2 hours. Remove and let cool.
5. In a saucepan, heat the demi-glace to a simmer and add
    wine and mushrooms. Cook for 20 minutes; keep warm.
6. One hour before serving pheasant, place in baking pan and
    cover with cabernet sauce; cover pan with plastic wrap,
    then foil. Heat to serving temperature in a 325°F oven.
7. Serve with steamed fresh vegetables and wild rice.
    Serves 8 to 12

Smoked Wild Turkey

From *Get Smokin'* by Cookshack, Inc.
© 2000 by Cookshack, Inc. Reprinted by permission of
Running Press, a member of Perseus Books, L.L.C.

Instructions

Split a 17-to 18-pound turkey into halves. Season with favorite chicken rub or a mixture of garlic, onion powder, celery powder, salt, and cayenne pepper to taste. Marinate in apple cider overnight. Smoke-cook with apple wood at 255°F for 4 to 5 hours. Wild turkey may be basted with Worcestershire sauce to give it a golden color. To reduce skin cracking, increase oven humidity with a Water Magazine (recommended from Cookshack) or rub with mayonnaise, butter, or vegetable oil before placing in smoker. Wild turkeys are sometimes as large as 27 pounds. Extend cooking time if smoking a larger bird.

Serves 14 to 16

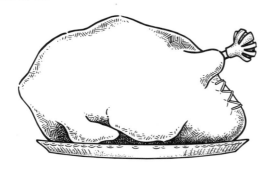

Vegetable Kebabs

Big Daddy's Confession: I've always hated vegetables! (Just ask my mother, whom I once caught sneaking carrot juice into my milk shake.) But when I tried grilled veggies, my opinion turned 180°. Barbecuing vegetables softens their texture, accentuates their sweetness, and imparts a smoky, nutty taste that I can't resist. In fact, I usually make veggie kebabs whenever I fire up the grill; they're a great side dish to anything. The flavor is even better when I throw some fruitwood or mesquite chips onto the coals. Many different vegetables work with this recipe, including yellow squash and cherry tomatoes. Or put two or three chunks of beef or lamb on the skewer to create a more nutritionally balanced and carnivore-friendly kebab.

1 small eggplant (about 3/4 pound) cut into 2-inch cubes

3 medium carrots, sliced into 1/2-inch pieces

8 small red potatoes, unpeeled

3 medium zucchini, sliced into 1-inch pieces

1 large bell pepper, red or green, seeded and cut into 1-inch squares

2 medium yellow onions, cut into wedges

16 mushrooms, whole

Bottled herb marinade, any brand

Salt and pepper to taste

8 metal skewers

1. Cook eggplant in 1 inch of boiling water for 3 minutes and drain. Cook carrots in 1 inch of boiling water until just tender-crisp and drain. Cook potatoes in 1 inch of boiling water for 15 to 20 minutes until soft. Drain and cut each potato in half. Separate onion wedges into 2 to 3 layer-wedges.

2. Place eggplant, carrots, potatoes, zucchini, peppers, onions, and mushrooms in a large zip-seal bag. Add marinade, seal bag well, and refrigerate for 2 hours or overnight.

3. Drain vegetables and reserve marinade. Using 8 metal skewers, thread vegetables, alternating varieties. Place on lightly greased grill over low heat. Cook, turning often, basting with the reserved marinade for 10 to 15 minutes until vegetables are tender and slightly charred around the edges. Sprinkle lightly with salt before serving. Remaining marinade can be refrigerated for up to 2 weeks. Note: If using bamboo skewers, soak them in water for 30 minutes first to prevent burning.

Serves 4

Beer-Steamed Sausages

Those who like a strong beer taste will want the sausage pieces that actually bathed in the beer. The pieces toward the top of the slow cooker will have a more delicate beery tang. During the 2 hours of cooking, the alcohol in the beer evaporates completely, so the whole family can enjoy this simple yet tasty dish.

Smoked sausage, enough to fill a slow cooker

1 can beer, room temperature, any brand

Cut each pound of smoked sausage into 4 pieces. Pour the beer into the slow cooker and pile in the sausage. Cook on High for 2 hours, then turn to Low until ready to serve.

Serves 4

I Burned Mine— Venison Summer Sausage

We sampled this tasty venison sausage at a competition, but in all our running around we not only failed to get the recipe for it, we couldn't even remember who made it. It wasn't until we started talking about how good it was after we got home that we realized we had to have it for the book, so we looked at the official map of teams for the event and mentally retraced our steps until we narrowed down where it came from. After several random e-mails we found Dave Higgins, Bruce Fischbach, and their team: I Burned Mine (I.B.M. for short). Any sausage good enough to get you to e-mail total strangers looking for how to make it must be good.

2 pounds ground venison
1 pound ground pork or Italian
  sausage
1/3 cup water
1 teaspoon salt
1 1/2 teaspoons McCormick's
  seasoning salt
1 teaspoon dry mustard

2 teaspoons mixed ground pepper
  (black, white, cayenne)
1/2 teaspoon garlic powder
1/4 teaspoon sugar
1/4 teaspoon liquid smoke
1 teaspoon fennel
1 small packet quick cure (can be
  purchased at Cabela's)

1. In a large bowl, thoroughly mix all the ingredients and shape into two equal-size logs.
2. Place in a smoker for 2 1/2 hours at 190°F to 220°F, or in the oven, on a rack with a drip pan, and bake at 300°F degrees for 1 hour.
3. Serve hot or cold. Slices better cold, but great either way. Refrigerate or freeze leftovers.
   Serves 6 to 8

The next three recipes are all from our old friend Remus Powers. I swear, when Remus writes about barbecue, I'm like Pavlov's dog outside a cathedral at high noon on Sunday.

Remus Powers' Brunswick Stew

There are at least as many versions of Brunswick stew as there are of meat loaf. Sometimes it's called burgoo, a close cousin that usually includes mutton or lamb. There was a time in the distant past when there were discernible differences between the two, like lamb for burgoo and squirrel for Brunswick stew. Nowadays burgoo and Brunswick stew are like a rumor that has been passed along so many times that there's at best a faint resemblance to the original. Unlike a rumor, however, this

Southern favorite will satisfy a hearty appetite and sustain you on a cold winter day. It's also a good way to use your leftover brisket and butt.

2 cups chopped sweet (Vidalia, if you can get them) onions
2 red or green bell peppers, seeded and chopped
1 cup chopped fresh carrots
1/4 cup bacon grease
1 pound boneless, skinless chicken breast, chopped
1 pound barbecue pork butt, chopped
1 pound barbecue brisket, chunked
2 cans (15 ounces each) crushed tomatoes
1 can (15 ounces) creamed corn
2 cans (15 ounces each) kernel corn
2 cans (15 ounces each) red beans, drained and rinsed

1 package (14 to 16 ounces) frozen lima beans
4 cups hot water
2 teaspoons Texas Pete, Louisiana, Red Devil, Frank's RedHot, Jump Up and Kiss Me, Scorned Woman, Tabasco hot sauce, or another of your favorites (Add more if you like extra fire.)
2 tablespoons apple cider vinegar
1 tablespoon freshly squeezed lemon juice
1/2 cup (1 stick) butter
1/2 cup whiskey (you can't go wrong with Jack Daniel's Old No. 7, green or black label)

I also like to add a cup or so of Johnny Harris Original Bar-B-Que Sauce, from Savannah, Georgia. Do it if you can get it.

1. In a large stew pot, sauté onion, peppers, and carrots in bacon grease until tender.
2. Add chicken breast and cook until done.
3. Add pork and beef; stir, then slowly add remaining ingredients. Stir with a wooden spoon and use low heat to avoid scorching the stew. You can start sampling after it simmers for an hour. It gets better with age, so the longer it simmers, the better the flavor. Adjust seasonings after each hour of simmering; thin with beer or water if necessary.

Serves about 10

Remus Powers's West African Groundnut Barbecue Stew

Original groundnut stew recipes in West Africa and elsewhere do not include barbecue meat, although some recipes call for grilled or smoked fish. This recipe is adapted from one given to me by a friend from Sierra Leone.

1 medium onion, chopped
1 small eggplant, peeled and cubed
4 to 5 mushrooms, sliced
1/4 cup canola oil
1 small can tomato paste
1/2 teaspoon sea salt
Pinch hot pepper
1 pound barbecued chicken meat, no bones or skin, chopped
1/2 pound barbecued beef brisket, cubed or chopped
1/2 pound barbecued pork butt, chopped
4 heaping tablespoons smooth peanut butter
1/2 cup chicken broth

1. In a large stew pot, sauté vegetables in oil. When vegetables are golden brown, add tomato paste, sea salt, and pepper. Stir, reduce heat, cover and simmer for 5 to 10 minutes.
2. Add all meats, stir ingredients, and simmer another 5 to 10 minutes.
3. In a separate bowl, mix peanut butter with chicken broth; stir with a fork or whisk until thoroughly blended; add to other ingredients in the pot and stir. Simmer for 5 to 10 minutes or until stew is thickened. Add salt or other seasonings and more peanut butter as needed.
4. Serve in a bowl over hot cooked rice.
   Serves about 6

Remus Powers's Poor Folks' BBQ Baloney

There was a time when chicken wings, ribs, beef brisket, and pork shoulder were cheap and undervalued. When spicy mambo wings and Buffalo wings went national in popularity, chicken wings suddenly became pricey. Likewise, as the barbecue method of cooking rendered ribs, brisket, and shoulder tasty, tender, and delicious, prices went up. Baloney became the last affordable meat option for poor folks. Cheap baloney sandwiches became a staple in blue-collar lunch pails across America.

The plain baloney sandwich was workweek fare, but come the weekend there was time to put a different spin on traditional baloney flavor. There was time to barbecue. I know this was done in Oklahoma, where I grew up, and I know it was done in Texas, and is still a standard barbecue item in both states. Texans also barbecue a smaller, spicier sausage they call hot links.

Barbecuing baloney is easy. Try my way first, then experiment with how you could make it better—perhaps by injecting it with a variety of liquid seasonings.

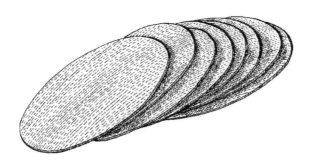

1 baloney tube (24 ounces)
Half a chimney of charcoal briquettes
(about 30)

1 handful of hardwood chips, soaked
for at least 30 minutes in water;
I like pecan but have also had
good results with hickory and
apple wood.
Nonstick cooking spray

1. Remove outer wrapping of baloney tube; puncture the baloney with a dinner fork, from end to end and all around. Not only can this give you cathartic relief from workplace stress, it will provide escape routes for baloney grease that would otherwise build up enough pressure to split your baloney. Split baloney is OK to eat, it just doesn't look as good.

2. Ignite briquettes and place them on one end of your fire grate. When coals are covered with gray ash, drain excess water off the wood chips and place them directly on the hot coals.

3. Spray your grill with cooking spray before placing it in the cooker. Place the baloney opposite the hot coals, lid your smoker, and cook the baloney at 200°F to 250°F for 1 hour.

4. Serve in chunks or slices with sauce on the side, or slice for sandwiches or cracker topper appetizers. Offer your guests a sweet tomato-based sauce and a spicy mustard-based sauce, and encourage them to try both. *Makes 6 servings with a meal or a platter full of servings on crackers*

9
Salads and Sides

Great barbecue is made even greater when served with one of these salads or side dishes. These recipes will come in handy when you're invited to a potluck barbecue party. Your friends will be pleasantly surprised, especially if your MO is to bring garden-variety macaroni salad from the deli.

Cold Potato Salad

6 large potatoes, peeled and quartered
1/3 cup oil, canola or olive
1 medium yellow onion, minced
3 teaspoons vinegar

1 teaspoon sugar
1/2 teaspoon prepared mustard
2 teaspoons dried dill weed, or chopped fresh dill

1. In a medium saucepan, cook potatoes in boiling, salted water until tender. Drain, reserving 3/4 cup of potato water. Dice potatoes; place in a large bowl. Add oil and onion; toss gently.
2. In a small saucepan, bring the reserved potato water to a boil; pour over potatoes and onion. Let stand at room temperature for 2 to 3 hours.

3. Stir in vinegar, sugar, mustard, and dill. Potato salad will be creamy. Serve at room temperature.
   Serves 6

Hot Potato Salad with Bacon

6 baking potatoes (about 2 pounds)
1 cup chopped onion
3 tablespoons chopped fresh parsley
1 teaspoon salt
1/4 teaspoon black pepper
2/3 cup white vinegar

1/3 cup water
1 1/2 teaspoons sugar
1 egg
1/3 cup oil, canola or olive
6 strips bacon, cooked to crisp

1. Scrub the potatoes and place in pot with enough water to cover. Cover and boil gently about 25 to 30 minutes until tender. Drain potatoes and shake pot over low heat to dry potatoes. Peel and cut into about 1/4-inch pieces. Place potatoes in a large bowl and toss with onions, parsley, salt, and pepper.
2. Combine vinegar, water, sugar in a small pan; heat to boiling.
3. In a small bowl, beat the egg slightly with a wire whisk. Continue beating while slowly pouring in the vinegar mixture. Slowly pour in the oil, whisking constantly.
4. Immediately pour this mixture over the warm potatoes and stir to coat evenly. Place the potatoes into a large skillet over low heat until heated throughout. Crumble bacon over potatoes. Serve immediately.
   Serves 6

Remus Powers's Sassy Sweet Down-South Coleslaw

Another favorite from Remus Powers

Finding a barbecue restaurant that doesn't serve coleslaw is as rare as finding a Bama fan wearing Tennessee Vol orange on game day. Some restaurants serve sweet slaw, some serve it tangy, and some serve it with a fiery bite to it.

Order a chopped or pulled pork sandwich in the South and, with few exceptions, your sandwich will come with a portion of slaw slapped atop the meat. Give in and take a bite. After that first bite you'll never want a pork sandwich any other way.

Since pork is sweet, the best slaw complement is a tangy slaw. This recipe is typical of many Southern slaw recipes in that it marries apple cider vinegar with sugar for a perfect mix of sweet and tangy, leaning to the tangy side. You can slap it onto a pulled pork sandwich or serve it as a side dish with a variety of barbecue meats.

SLAW:
1 bag (16 ounces) coleslaw; OR
1/2 head cabbage, chopped
1/2 cup chopped onion
1/2 cup chopped red, green, or orange bell pepper

DRESSING:
1/2 cup sugar
1 teaspoon sea salt
1 pinch celery seed
1/2 cup apple cider vinegar
1 cup canola oil
1/2 cup prepared yellow mustard

1. Place coleslaw in a large bowl
2. Put dry dressing ingredients in a lidded quart jar. Add

vinegar and shake until absorbed. Add oil and mustard; shake lidded jar until dressing binds.

3. Pour dressing on slaw right before serving, and toss until coated. Entire jar may not be needed for one bag of slaw; adjust amount used to your taste.

Serves 6

Grilled Chicken and Apple Salad

1 pound boneless, skinless chicken breast halves
1 package Betty Crocker Suddenly Salad classic pasta salad mix
1/3 cup mayonnaise

1/4 cup apple juice
1 large apple, red Delicious or Granny Smith, cored and thinly sliced
1/2 cup pecans, chopped (optional)

1. Put chicken on oiled grill 4 to 6 inches from medium heat, lower barbecue cover, and cook for 15 to 20 minutes, turning often, until chicken is golden brown and juices run clear. Let cool.

2. While chicken is grilling, fill a large saucepan 2/3 full of water and boil. Stir in contents of pasta-vegetable pouch of pasta salad mix. Gently boil uncovered for 12 minutes, stirring occasionally, until tender. Drain pasta and rinse with cold water. Shake to drain well.

3. In a large bowl, combine the seasoning mix, mayonnaise, and apple juice. Cut chicken into 2 x 1/2-inch strips. Stir the chicken, pasta, and apple into seasoning mixture.

4. Just before serving, toss with Suddenly Salad topping; sprinkle with chopped pecans, if desired. Cover and refrigerate leftovers; keeps for 48 hours.

Serves 4

Grilled Chicken Breast and Bean Salad

2 to 3 tablespoons spicy mustard
4 boneless, skinless chicken breast halves
1 package (10-ounces) frozen black-eyed peas
32 ounces canned beans, combination of kidney, garbanzo, and white
1 medium-large red onion, finely chopped
2 medium-large ripe tomatoes, coarsely chopped
4 sun-dried tomato halves, in oil, finely chopped
2 to 3 tablespoons chopped fresh thyme
2 to 3 tablespoons chopped fresh oregano
3 tablespoons extra-virgin olive oil
3 tablespoons balsamic vinegar
Freshly ground black pepper to taste

1. Heat broiler or prepare outdoor grill. Spread the mustard on one side of the chicken breasts and broil or grill until they begin to brown. Turn and spread on additional mustard. Cook until done. Cut chicken into narrow strips and place in serving bowl.
2. Cook the peas according to package directions, not more than 15 minutes; drain. Drain liquid from canned beans and rinse thoroughly. In a large bowl, combine the beans, peas, onion, fresh and dried tomatoes, thyme, and oregano.
3. Beat the oil and vinegar together; mix into salad ingredients and season with pepper. Serve at room temperature.

Serves 6

Grilled Chicken Salad with Roasted Garlic Dressing

4 boneless, skinless chicken breast halves

2/3 cup plus 4 teaspoons bottled marinade (such as Kikkoman Quick & Easy Marinades Roasted Garlic & Herbs)

2 tablespoons freshly squeezed lemon juice

1 teaspoon sugar

1/2 cup oil, canola or extra-virgin olive

Mixed salad greens

1. In a large zip-seal bag, put the chicken and 2/3 cup of marinade. Close bag and marinate in the refrigerator for 20 minutes, turning chicken over once.
2. Meanwhile, in a small bowl, make the dressing by mixing 4 teaspoons of marinade with the lemon juice and sugar; whisk in oil gradually; set aside.
3. Remove chicken from bag; reserve marinade. Grill or broil chicken 5 to 6 inches from the heat source for 8 minutes. Turn chicken over, brush with marinade, and cook 6 to 7 minutes more, or until there's no pink left in the center of the breasts. Slice chicken into 1/2-inch strips; arrange on salad greens and serve with the lemon-oil dressing.

Serves 4

Grilled Steak Caesar Salad

If you are short on time, the marinade may be used as a brush-on glaze. Brush liberally on steak while grilling.

1/2 cup A.1. Steak Sauce, Original or Bold & Spicy
3 tablespoons freshly squeezed lemon juice
1 teaspoon minced anchovy fillets
1 teaspoon minced garlic

1/2 cup olive oil, extra-virgin or mild
1 boneless beef top-round steak, about 1 pound and 1 inch thick
4 cups torn romaine lettuce leaves
1 cup croutons
2 ounces Parmesan cheese, shaved

1. In a small bowl, blend the steak sauce, lemon juice, anchovy, and garlic; slowly whisk in oil. Place steak in nonmetal dish or zip-seal bag; add 1/3 cup steak-sauce marinade. Cover and refrigerate 1 hour, turning meat occasionally. Reserve remaining marinade for dressing.
2. Remove steak from marinade; discard used marinade with bag. Grill steak over medium-high heat for 6 minutes per each side or until desired doneness. Heat reserved dressing until warm.
3. Spread lettuce leaves on serving platter. Thinly slice steak; arrange on lettuce. Drizzle with warm dressing; top with croutons and cheese.
    Serves 4

Grandpa's Famous Roasting Corn

I remember as a boy romping around my grandpa's farm on summer Sundays, hangin' with the hogs, chasin' the chickens, and throwing hay at my sister. But my fondest memory is Grandpa's famous roasting corn. He kept the recipe locked in his shotgun cabinet, but I broke in—for the recipe, not the guns! (Sorry, Grandpa, but it's too darn good to keep to yourself!)

8 cobs of corn, fresh, husks intact   1/2 teaspoon salt
1/2 cup (1 stick) butter or margarine   Dash chili powder
Juice from 2 limes

1. Prepare a medium-hot fire (same as cooking steaks). Dampen the husks and, if desired, wrap in foil. Grill for 15 to 20 minutes, turning to roast both sides. When ready to serve, remove husks and coat with butter, lime juice, salt, and chili powder.
   Serves 8

Budha's Baked Beans

You knew this one was coming, straight from Budha himself: "Damned good and musical too!"

This recipe is a great use of the extra bits that you have from cooked briskets, pork butts and or ribs. You can buy the Gate's sauces at www.gatesbbq.com. If I am not cooking a batch of beans, I will keep the bits from any meats that I smoke and freeze them for future use.

2 cans (15 ounces each) ranch-style beans with jalapeños

1 1/2 cups packed light brown sugar

3/4 cup Budha's All Purpose Meat Rub (see page 17)

9 ounces (1/2 bottle) Gate's Sweet and Mild BBQ Sauce

9 ounces (1/2 bottle) Gate's Extra Hot BBQ Sauce

1 diced medium Vidalia onion

1 pound prepared brisket, pork butt, or rib pieces

1. In a 1/2 inch-deep aluminum pan, combine all the ingredients.
2. If meat is not prepared yet, place pan in smoker while you are cooking your brisket, pork butt, or ribs, and add meat bits to the beans as they become available. Stir occasionally, and cook uncovered at 225°F for at least 3 hours—the longer, the better.

Serves 10 to 12

Jennifer's Mac 'n' Cheese

My neighbor Jennifer has more than good looks to draw me into her kitchen. Her version of macaroni and cheese gives a gourmet's touch to this kiddy comfort food.

2 cups uncooked elbow macaroni
3 tablespoons butter or margarine
1 small yellow onion, finely chopped
2 tablespoons all-purpose flour
1 teaspoon dry mustard

1 teaspoon salt
1/4 teaspoon black pepper
2 cups milk
2 1/2 cups shredded Cheddar cheese

TOPPING:
1 crusty roll, sourdough or French
2 tablespoons butter

3/4 cup shredded Cheddar cheese

1. Preheat oven to 375°F. Butter a casserole dish (I use one that's about 12 inches square); set aside.
2. Cook macaroni according to package directions.
3. In a large saucepan, melt 3 tablespoons of the butter. Add onion and cook until tender. Stir in flour, mustard, salt, and pepper. Add milk slowly, stirring constantly, and cook until sauce is thickened and bubbly. Add 2 1/2 cups of cheese and stir until melted. Combine cooked macaroni and cheese mixture and mix well. Pour into prepared dish.
4. To make topping, tear roll apart and use steel blade of food processor to chop into fine bread crumbs. In a small saucepan, melt the 2 tablespoons of butter; add crumbs and toss until covered. Combine buttered crumbs with the 3/4 cup of cheese; spread over casserole.
5. Bake for 20 to 25 minutes, until topping is nicely browned and macaroni is bubbly.
Serves 6

10
Drinks

There's nothing like a special drink as a cool counterpoint to a hot barbecue meal. In this chapter, you'll find everything you need to prepare the perfect liquid companion for your outdoor feast.

Beer

6-pack beer, your favorite brand

1. Chill.
2. Remove from refrigerator.
3. Open can or bottle.
4. Pour into frosted mug (optional).
5. Repeat.

Big Daddy Lowdown: Once chilled, beer that is allowed to return to room temperature is said to have "skunked." With a foul odor and bitter aftertaste, skunked beer should be avoided at all costs. On a more serious note, regardless of how fresh your beer is, drinking it before getting behind the wheel of your vehicle should be avoided as well.

11
Sweet Endings

What's a meal without a great dessert? Not much, my mother would say. So here are some of my favorite dessert recipes, most of them courtesy of Big Daddy's Mama. Some old friends manage to kick in one or two.

Fluffy Fruit Salad

This creamy alternative to the garden-variety fruit salad is a real crowd-pleaser.

2 20-ounce cans crushed pineapple
2/3 cup sugar
2 tablespoons flour
2 eggs, lightly beaten
1/4 cup orange juice
3 tablespoons lemon juice
1 tablespoon oil, canola or olive

2 17-ounce cans fruit cocktail, drained
2 11-ounce cans Mandarin, orange slices, drained
2 bananas, sliced
1 cup heavy cream, whipped

1. Drain pineapple, reserving 1 cup of the juice in a small saucepan. Set pineapple aside.
2. In a medium saucepan, combine sugar, flour, eggs, orange juice, lemon juice, and oil. Bring to a boil,

stirring constantly. Boil for 1 minute; remove from heat and let cool.

3. In a salad bowl, combine the pineapple, fruit cocktail, oranges, and bananas. Fold in whipped cream and cooled sauce. Refrigerate several hours before serving. *Serves 6*

Jimmy Carter Dessert

Remember the jokes about Jimmy Carter being a peanut farmer? Yeah? Boy, you're old! At any rate, this multi-layered tribute to our former president from Georgia should be removed from the freezer 1 hour before serving. Refrigerate or refreeze any leftovers.

1 1/2 cups chopped peanuts
1 cup all-purpose flour
1/2 cup (1 stick) butter or margarine, softened
8 ounces cream cheese, softened
1 cup 10X (confectioners') sugar
1 1/2 cups whipped topping (12 ounces)

1/2 cup smooth peanut butter
1 small package instant chocolate pudding
1 small package instant vanilla pudding
2 1/2 cups milk, cold
1 cup chocolate syrup

1. In a bowl, mix 1 cup of the peanuts with the flour and butter or margarine. Blend and press in 13 x 9-inch pan to make crust. Bake 20 minutes at 300°F. Cool.
2. Using an electric mixer on slow setting, cream the cream cheese with the powdered sugar and peanut butter. Using a spoon, add 1 cup of the whipped topping and blend. Carefully spread mixture onto the cooled crust.
3. Blend chocolate and vanilla puddings into cold milk; mix well. Spread on top of first layer.

4. Spread remaining 1/2 cup of whipped topping on top of pudding layer.
5. Drizzle chocolate syrup on top of whipped topping.
6. Sprinkle with remaining 1/2 cup of chopped peanuts. Freeze.

    Serves 10

Old-Fashioned Peach Cobbler

The easiest way to peel a fresh peach is to score the stem and place it whole into boiling water for about 1 minute or until the skin softens up. Using a slotted spoon, transfer the peaches to a bowl of cold water. When cooled, the peels will come off without a fight.

1/2 cup packed light brown sugar
1/2 teaspoon cinnamon, ground
1 teaspoon lemon zest (grated lemon peel)
1 tablespoon lemon juice
4 cups fresh peaches, peeled and sliced
3/4 cup all-purpose flour

1/2 cup whole-wheat flour
1 tablespoon baking powder
1/4 cup (1/2 stick) butter, softened
2 egg whites, beaten
1/2 cup milk
1/2 teaspoon vanilla
Whipped cream or vanilla ice cream

1. Preheat oven to 375°F. Lightly grease 8 x 8 x 2-inch baking dish.
2. In a large bowl, combine brown sugar, cinnamon, lemon rind, and lemon juice. Add peaches; toss to mix. Transfer to prepared baking dish.
3. Combine flours and baking powder on a piece of waxed paper.
4. In a medium-size bowl beat together butter and sugar until light and fluffy. Beat in egg whites. Add flour mixture alternately with milk and vanilla, stirring just to combine.

5. Drop batter by spoonfuls over peach mixture. Spread gently. Bake 25 to 30 minutes, or until peaches are tender and crust is golden brown. Serve warm with dollop of whipped topping or vanilla ice cream.
    Serves 8

Grasshopper Pie

Don't worry, there aren't any grasshoppers in it—unless you want to add some (for the protein, and the crunch). For the best results, use a candy thermometer (not a meat thermometer) when preparing the custard. You can make the chocolate crumbs yourself by putting a couple handfuls of chocolate wafers in a zip-seal bag and having at it with a hammer.

1 1/2 cups chocolate wafer crumbs, fine (Nabisco Nilla or other brand)
1/4 cup sugar

1/4 cup (1/2 stick) unsalted butter, softened

CUSTARD FILLING:
1 1/2 teaspoons unflavored gelatin
1 1/3 cups heavy cream, chilled
1/4 cup sugar

1/4 cup green crème de menthe
1/4 cup white crème de cacao
4 large egg yolks

GARNISH:
Mint-flavored chocolate, grated

1. Preheat oven to 450°F. Grease a 9-inch pie plate with butter.
2. In a medium bowl, stir together the wafer crumbs, sugar, and butter until the mixture is combined well. Pat the mixture onto the bottom and sides of the buttered pie plate. Bake in the middle of the oven for 5 minutes. Let it cool completely.

3. In a metal bowl, sprinkle the gelatin over 1/3 cup of the cream and let it soften for 5 minutes. Whisk in the sugar, crème de menthe, crème de cacao, and egg yolks. Set the bowl over a saucepan of simmering water, and cook the mixture, whisking constantly, until it measures 160°F on a candy thermometer. Transfer the bowl of custard to an ice-water bath, and stir until cooled and thickened.

4. In another bowl, beat the remaining cup of cream until it holds stiff peaks. Fold it into the custard thoroughly, until no streaks of white remain.

5. Pour the filling into the crust, and chill the pie for at least 4 hours, or until it is set. Sprinkle with grated chocolate and serve.

    Serves 6

Candy Bars

1ST LAYER:
1 cup milk-chocolate chips

1/4 cup butterscotch chips

2ND LAYER:
1 cup sugar
1/4 cup milk
1/4 cup (1/2 stick) margarine
1/4 cup smooth peanut butter

1 cup marshmallow cream (Fluff or
  other brand)
1 teaspoon vanilla extract
2 cups peanuts

3RD LAYER:
40 caramels, unwrapped

2 tablespoons water

4TH LAYER:
1 cup milk-chocolate chips
1/4 cup butterscotch chips

1/4 cup smooth peanut butter

1. Grease a 13 x 9-inch pan; set aside. In a saucepan, over low heat, melt ingredients for first layer and spread in prepared pan. Freeze until firm.
2. In a saucepan, boil the sugar, milk, and margarine for 5 minutes. Stir in the peanut butter, marshmallow cream, and vanilla. Pour over the first layer and sprinkle with peanuts. Cool.
3. In a saucepan, melt the caramels with the water and pour over the second layer.
4. In a saucepan, melt the chips and peanut butter together. Pour over the third layer. Refrigerate 1 to 2 hours. Cut into squares.

Serves 12

Southern Pumpkin Pecan Roll

This recipe is somewhat complicated, although well worth the effort. I suggest a trial run before making it for your next barbecue party.

3/4 cup cake flour
1 teaspoon baking powder
1/4 teaspoon salt
2 teaspoons ground cinnamon
1 teaspoon ground ginger
1/2 teaspoon ground nutmeg
3 eggs, separated
3/4 cup packed light brown sugar

1/4 cup canned pumpkin, solid pack (Libby's or other brand)
2 pints ice cream, any flavor, slightly softened
1/2 cup dark corn syrup
Clean towel, lightly dusted with powdered sugar
1 1/2 cups pecan halves

1. Preheat oven to 350°F. Grease and flour a 15 x 10 x 1-inch jelly-roll pan. Line with greased and floured wax paper: set aside.
2. In a small bowl, combine flour, baking powder, salt, cinnamon, ginger, and nutmeg; set aside.

3. In a large mixing bowl, beat egg yolks until thick, about 5 minutes. Gradually add the brown sugar; beat well. Stir in the pumpkin. Gradually add the dry ingredients; beat until smooth.

4. In a small mixing bowl, beat egg whites until stiff peaks form. Fold into batter. Spread evenly into prepared pan. Bake for 15 to 18 minutes, or until top springs back when lightly touched. Immediately loosen sides of cake. Invert onto towel. Remove waxed paper. Fold one end of towel over narrow end of cake; roll cake in towel. Cool on wire rack.

5. When the cake is completely cooled, unroll and spread with ice cream to within 1/2 inch of edges. Reroll, using towel to guide cake and keep it round and firm. With seam side down, freeze until firm.

6. In a small saucepan, bring corn syrup to a boil. Boil gently for about 2 minutes, stirring constantly, until syrup slightly thickens. Cool for 1 minute.

7. Liberally brush corn syrup over frozen cake roll. Press pecan halves in even rows over surface. Cover with plastic wrap. Return to freezer.

8. To serve, cut into 1-inch slices. Let slices stand 10 minutes before eating.

Serves 4

Chocolate Chip Cookies with a Cayenne Kick

No supercomputers here—in addition to sweet summer sausages, the I.B.M. team also makes a mean cookie, the kind that spills its own milk and scares off Santa. They pulled this one straight from the newspaper years ago, and we sure are glad they did, 'cause our burning taste buds haven't been the same since. It's a variation on the original Toll House chocolate chip cookie recipe, reprinted here with permission from Nestlé.

2 1/4 cups all-purpose flour	1 teaspoon vanilla extract
1 teaspoon baking soda	2 large eggs
1 teaspoon salt	2 cups Nestlé Toll House
1 cup (2 sticks) butter or margarine, softened	Semi-Sweet Chocolate Morsels
3/4 cup granulated sugar	1 cup chopped nuts
3/4 cup packed brown sugar	2-4 tablespoons of powdered cayenne pepper (to taste)

1. Preheat oven to 375°F.
2. In a small bowl, combine the flour, baking soda, and salt. In a large mixing bowl, beat the butter, granulated sugar, brown sugar, and vanilla extract until creamy. Add eggs one at a time, beating well after each addition. Gradually beat in flour mixture. Stir in morsels, nuts, and cayenne pepper. Drop by rounded tablespoons onto ungreased baking sheets.
3. Bake for 9 to 11 minutes in preheated oven, until golden brown. Cool on baking sheets for 2 minutes; transfer to wire racks to cool completely.

Makes about 5 dozen cookies

Big Mama's Sweet Potato Pie

Doc Remus did us the honor of opening our book, so we couldn't think of a better way to close it out than with this Southern favorite.

When the barbecue is good, you may be too full for dessert. If sweet potato pie is on the menu, however, you'd best save room for it. Some barbecue restaurants–but too few as far as I'm concerned—offer sweet potato pie. If you can't get it at your favorite rib shack, try Big Mama's recipe. It's easy and delicious.

1 pound fresh sweet potatoes
2 farm-fresh eggs, beaten (cage-free egg yolks are richer in color)
1 1/4 cups evaporated milk
3/4 cup packed brown sugar
1/2 teaspoon kosher or sea salt

1 1/2 teaspoons ground cinnamon
1 teaspoon freshly grated nutmeg
3 tablespoons butter, melted
1 9-inch deep pie crust (I take the easy way and buy a frozen crust)

1. Preheat oven to 425°F. Peel potatoes, rinse them under fresh running water, then slice into inch-thick pieces.
2. Put potatoes in a medium-size pot and add enough water to cover them. Add a pinch of salt, put the lid on the pot, and bring to a boil. Reduce to simmer for about 20 minutes until potatoes are soft.
3. Remove potatoes from water, and place in a large bowl. Mash them, then add eggs, milk, brown sugar, salt, spices, and melted butter. Mix until there are no lumps; pour mixture into pie crust.
4. Place pie in preheated oven. After 10 minutes, turn heat down to 300°F; bake 50 minutes or until done.
Serves 8

Photograph courtesy of Frank Boyer

Acknowledgments

Robin K. Levinson played a big part in putting this project together—many thanks to her for her efforts. Additional thanks to everyone at Chamberlain Bros.: Carlo DeVito, Ron Martirano, Jeanette Shaw, Mike Rivilis, Meredith Phebus, Elizabeth Wagner, and Cherisse Dike.

Thanks to the following sources, for allowing us to reprint their material:

- Anthony Watson at Mountain Software for his Home Cookin' recipes
- Cookshack, Inc.
- Evie Hansen, from *Seafood Grilling Twice a Week*
- Michael Greenwald, from *The Cruisin' Chef Cookbook*
- Nestlé Toll House Cookies

Finally, it goes without saying that a collection of recipes cannot exist without those willing to share their love of good food and their knowledge as to how it gets made. In addition to the dozens of people in Iowa, Kansas, and across the country who were hospitable enough to talk with us (and allow us to sample their entries), we would like to thank the following contributors:

- Ardie Davis, aka Remus Powers, Ph.B.
- Budha Mangus, aka Rick Stofer
- I Burned Mine—Bruce Fischbach, David Higgins, and Rosemary Hume
- River City Rubs—Simon Guzman and Theron Malone
- Smitty's Bar-B-Que—Brian Smith, Patrick Smith, Dan Sobek, and Eric Johnson